Religion and Power Decline and Growth:

Sociological analyses of religion in Britain, Poland and the Americas

edited by

Peter Gee
and
John Fulton

British Sociological Association
Sociology of Religion Study Group

Acknowledgements
Thanks are due to the Overseas Development Institute for permitting the use of their computers and printers in the production of this book, and to all those who assisted with proofing and correction of the text.

The chapters in this book are based on papers first given at the conference of the British Sociological Association Sociology of Religion Study Group held at Strawberry Hill in April 1989.

Chapter 5: 'Enjoying God Forever: an historical/sociological profile of the health and wealth gospel in the USA' by Dennis Hollinger was first published in a different form in *Trinity Journal* Volume 9 (2), Fall 1988, pp 131-149.

British Library Cataloguing in Publication Data is available on request.

Published by the British Sociological Association Sociology of Religion Study Group.

ISBN 0 9517224 0 9

Typeset in Century Schoolbook and prepared on disk using WordPerfect 5 by Peter Gee at the Overseas Development Institute, London.
Printed by Chameleon Press Ltd, London

Contents

Editors and Contributors

Editors

Dr John Fulton, Senior Lecturer, Department of Sociology, St Mary's College, Twickenham.
Dr Peter Gee, Publications and Information Technology Officer, Overseas Development Institute, London.

Contributors

Dr Anne Eyre, Lecturer, MARA College of Higher Education, Darul Khusus, Malaysia.
Professor Robin Gill, William Leech Fellow in Applied Christian Theology, University of Newcastle.
Dr Halina Grzymala-Moszczynska, Institute of Religious Studies, University of Krakow, Poland.
Dr Paul Heelas, Lecturer, Department of Religious Studies, University of Lancaster.
Dr Dennis Hollinger, Associate Professor, Goshen Biblical Seminary, Elkhart, Indiana, USA.
Dr Michael Hornsby-Smith, Senior Lecturer, Department of Sociology, University of Surrey, Guildford, Surrey.
Krzysztof Kosela, Institute of Sociology, University of Warsaw, Poland.
Dr Leonard Mars, Department of Sociology & Anthropology, University College of Swansea, Wales.
Margaret Norris, Honorary Visiting Fellow, Department of Sociology, University of Surrey, Guildford, Surrey.
Dr Burke Rochford,Jr, Associate Professor, Department of Sociology & Anthropology, Middlebury College, Middlebury, Vermont, USA.
Professor Kenneth Thompson, Faculty of Social Sciences, The Open University, Milton Keynes.
Dr Bryan Wilson, Reader in Sociology, University of Oxford.

Introduction

Since the disappearance of *The Sociological Yearbook of Religion in Britain* in the late seventies, sociologists working in Britain on the subject have had to go abroad to submit specialist articles or have been able to get local journals to accept their wares only when these have been perceived of general interest.

In this book, which may turn out to be biennial, we seek to remedy this situation, but within the framework of certain self-imposed limitations. Contributions are centred around a theme, thus making the book more specific in its contribution. Also, aware of the danger of an isolated British sociology of religion, we seek to make the presentation more comparative, embodying studies by overseas members of this particular study group of the British Sociological Association, and including research of subjects beyond national boundaries.

The present theme - religion and power, decline and growth - focuses on a subject frequently confined to two principal areas: the power of religion over group members and the decline of religion in contemporary societies, the so-called secularization thesis. While studies directly relevant to these two themes are present in this book, such as Thompson's critique of secularization theory and Gill's study of church building and population decline in nineteenth century North-East England, other dimensions are equally explored.

Within the British context, the growth of specific movements within Roman Catholicism (Hornsby-Smith, Fulton & Norris), the internal struggles and accommodation of Jewry to the Welsh environment (Mars), the coupling of religion with capitalism in the activity of the cult Exegesis / Programmes (Heelas) and the political battle over the use of religion to support Thatcherite trickle-down theory (Eyre) all indicate the wider economic and political frameworks within which religion operates. It is by articulating such relationships that sociology of religion is finding its way back into the central areas of sociological concern.

Studies outside of the British context reinforce this perspective, while viewing similar issues from within the different structural and cultural frames there at work. The growth of protestantism in Latin America (Wilson's examination of David Martin's work), the diversity of worldviews and the complexity of the political and religious powers operating in Poland (Grzymala-Moszczynska and Kosela), the factors at work in leaving and rejoining a contemporary cult in the U.S. (Rochford), the economic underpinnings and ideologies affecting the health and wealth gospel movement and similarly oriented cult forms in the U.S. (Hollinger and Heelas again), all strengthen the awareness of the broader frame. They direct reflection towards the key traditional insight of both Weber and Marx that sociological understanding of religion is flawed without an awareness of its economic and political aspects. If, in one perspective, religion is a source of charismatic social energy, in another it is also a source of political and economic activity which strengthens or challenges the dominant culture, be it communist or capitalist.

If one were to make a general comment on the contributions in this volume, it would be that the processes which religion undergoes and which are traditionally encompassed under the label of secularization are one side of a coin, on the other side of which is an ongoing engagement with a political, economic and other-cultural world in which religious institutions and movements are subjects. One could develop a term analogous to Durkheim's *homo duplex*, namely *religio duplex*, in which action and passion, power and secularization, growth and decline are seen as a succession of contrasting and opposite aspects or faces, in place of the duality of individual and society.

1
The Secularization Debate

Kenneth Thompson

Of the many contributions made by David Martin to the sociology of religion perhaps the most important is his contribution to the theory of secularization. In addition to providing us with outstanding cross-cultural studies, his contribution has been to explore some of the cultural and structural factors that limit or nullify the tendencies towards secularization in industrial societies.

In **A General Theory of Secularization** (1978) he listed 'certain broad tendencies towards secularization in industrial society' that amounted to 'a universal process'. They were as follows:

> that religious institutions are adversely affected to the extent that an area is dominated by heavy industry; that they are the more adversely affected if the area concerned is homogeneously proletarian; that religious practice declines proportionately with the size of an urban concentration; that geographical and social mobility erodes stable religious communities organized on a territorial basis; that it also contributes to relativization of perspectives through extended culture contact; that the church becomes institutionally differentiated in response to the differentiation of society, notably into pluriform denominations and sects; that the church becomes partially differentiated from other institutional spheres: such as justice, ideological legitimation, the state apparatus, social control, education, welfare; and this is paralleled by a compartmentalization of an individual's religious role which may encourage a range of variation in personal religion which contributes to institutional disintegration. (Martin 1978:3).

There are two sets of factors here: the first are what Durkheim called 'social morphological', concerned with population distribution and interaction e.g. concentration of population in areas of heavy industry, homogeneously proletarian, urban concentration and high mobility. The second set are concerned with institutional differentiation and the effect of this on culture - especially religious culture. Whereas there is empirical evidence that the first set of factors correlates fairly clearly with decline in religious belief and practice, the correlation of the second set with religious decline is much more speculative and deserves closer examination of the implicit assumptions about the nature of religion and secularization. Martin's major contribution has been to map out some of the cultural factors that limit secularization in different societies and it is this topic of culture and secularization that I want to suggest could be the most fruitful for developing the sociology of religion in new directions. However, his theory of secularization also raises a few questions about the inevitability of this process in relation to morphological or structural factors, and I will examine these first.

Structural factors

As an example of a structural limiting factor he mentions that 'the dominance of heavy industry (which certainly has deleterious effects on "religion") may be a diminishing characteristic of modern societies' (Martin 1978:2). Starting from this implicit notion of periodization — that 'modern' society is not a single stage of development with permanent characteristics — prompts us to question whether secularization should be regarded any more as a permanent feature of mature industrial societies, especially as these are increasingly spoken of as 'post-industrial' and 'post-modern'. As sociologists of religion we may have to alter our view of secularization, looking less to a past 'golden age' of religion to judge the present, and more to possible futures in the light of emerging trends. And rather than regarding America as an exception to a universal secularizing trend, we may have to entertain the possibility that, as in other social developments, it is the shape of one of the possible futures.

In other words, secularization may not be a universal process at all stages of development of industrial societies. Its association with features such as heavy industry suggests that it may be a trend limited to a particular stage of industrialization. In societies with mature economies, increasingly dominated by service industries and knowledge-based productive processes, with lower concentrations of workers in factories and more dispersed and even home-based work, secularization may be much less than in the period of large heavy industries, and it may even lose ground. The factor of heavy industry is also related to another factor affecting secularization — the extent to which an area is 'homogeneously proletarian' (Martin 1979:3). This is likely to be less and less the case in a post-industrial society. Societies with mature industrial economies tend to experience a movement out of the cities, leaving the cities to single people, childless couples and the poor who cannot afford to move. With the movement of families to small towns and extended villages outside the cities, the conditions are established for a revival of religion. Furthermore, this is a type of social mobility which does not necessarily promote secularization, unlike the earlier movement into cities or the movement of single people and childless couples between cities. (Furthermore, young single people are a fertile ground for sects, just as many of the inner city poor are drawn from minority ethnic groups which have relatively thriving religions). Nor does the newer form of geographical and social mobility inevitably contribute to a 'relativization of perspectives through extended culture contact': it is more likely to be marked by a desire to cultivate a sense of community. There is a potential here for a resurgence of religious community. Whether it occurs or not will depend on other factors, such as the capacity of the local church to capitalize on the opportunities and provide an adequate supply of religious professionals (e.g. the ordination of women might make a contribution to this). Certainly, if the economy does become more knowledge-based in its production processes, with a consequent decline of the old proletariat and a growth of the middle classes, there will no longer be a significant class barrier to church membership.

The second set of factors mentioned by David Martin, that of differentiation, both between religious organizations and between religion and other institutions, need not be damaging to religion per se, but possibly only to religion dependent on traditional forms and structures. Differentiation can also be liberating. Sects have always provided evidence of one such possibility. But increased organizational reforms in the church that facilitate flexibility and adaptability, provided they are 'market-sensitive', can also be productive. In post-industrial society, market-sensitivity means eschewing standardization and 'mass-production' in favour of providing services adapted to the requirements of individuals and groups. This should not be confused with 'modernizing' religion, in the discredited sense of substituting for traditional forms an up-to-date version. As in other spheres, such as housing design, tastes will vary, and may include a taste for nostalgia and a revival of older styles — the Latin Mass or the 1662 Prayer Book. The most inappropriate response is a centralized prescription of standardized modern forms. Theoretically (whether 'market theory' or 'post-modernist theory'), each local church, or group of churches in a locality, should be free to offer a range of products or services to suit as many tastes as possible, whilst seeking to avoid spreading confusion and unpredictability. It may be objected that this pluralization is a sign of secularization, but that is only the case if secularization is equated with differentiation and means nothing more than loss of homogeneity.

It can be argued that it is this kind of internal differentiation and pluralization in a national church like the Church of England that has enabled it to maintain its status as an ecclesia type of religious body, rather than becoming one denomination among others. It offers the most comprehensive range of 'services' to suit the most varied religious tastes — Catholic ritualism, conservative traditionalism, modernist, low church, evangelical, and charismatic. According to market theory, this should be a strength. Why then does it appear to be a weakness? One reason is that essentially the church is not simply a utilitarian, let alone a commercial, concern. Whenever it adopts instrumental or utilitarian criteria to rationalize its organizational functioning it is vulnerable to the charge that it is departing from its true vocation as a sacred entity. This was evident in the criticisms levelled by members of the Oxford Movement against the reforms of the Ecclesiastical Commissioners in the nineteenth century. They objected to the primacy given to formally rational criteria to the exclusion of considerations of tradition, divine ordinance, and symbolic appropriateness of the means employed in relation to transcendental values and ultimate ends. Thus to Pusey, the only criterion appropriate to discussions of cathedrals was their 'sacredness' and the Ecclesiastical Commission's application of the criteria of 'utility' seemed to him inappropriate (Thompson 1970:221).

This makes it very difficult for the church to capitalize on its comprehensiveness through rational planning to take account of different market requirements. For example, a rural deanery cannot plan to offer a range of services to suit demand in its geographical area, with a mix of different sorts of churchmanship (Anglo-Catholic, Evangelical, etc.), because churchmanship is viewed as a matter of sacred truth, not just a matter of catering to taste. Of course, in practice, there is a certain amount of compromise of principles to suit demand; clergymen to varying degrees do tailor the service to satisfy local tastes, and diocesan bishops try to find clergymen who they think will fit in with such preferences. However, there are limits to any rational planning which attempts to fit supply to demand and there is little market research to find out what local people (potential members) would like from the church. As for other aspects of what are regarded as 'secular' organizational techniques, such as those concerned with creating demand through advertising and promotion, these are extremely limited in most religious bodies outside America. The main criticisms of internal secularization of religious organizations are directed at the bureaucratic forms of financial organization, democratic representation, or the blurring of the boundary between the sacred and secular by too much involvement in contemporary secular matters, such as political and economic affairs (a favourite criticism levelled by Edward Norman and some critics of the Bishop of Durham). Such critics implicitly accept the relegation of the church to a sectarian body, which must preserve its separateness from the other institutions of secularized society. In effect they wish to accentuate the institutional separation of the sacred and profane for fear that contact with the latter can only pollute and dilute the integrity and potency of the sacred.

David Martin's most recent work on Latin American Protestantism has raised the question of whether the European experience was not so much evidence of a universal process of secularization as a contingent case involved with disintegration of religious monopoly. According to this alternative view:

> the effect of establishment and religious monopoly such as existed in Europe has been to inhibit the adaptability of religion to social change, above all to the industrial city. However, the North American paradigm seems to show that once religion is no longer a matter of a relation of a particular body to the elite and to the state, religion adapts quite successfully to a changing world. In all the proper senses of the word it becomes popular. Indeed, it shows itself endlessly inventive and actually succeeds in assuaging the anomie and combatting the chaos of the megacity (Martin, 1990:295)

The suggestion is that 'secularization as understood in the European context is a particular kind of episode. If there is a universal element to it that is restricted to the shift from structural location to cultural influence' (ibid).

Cultural factors

In other words, the change in the structural location of religion need not reduce the cultural viability and potency of religion. It might even free it to adapt and thrive. However, the remaining question is whether the cultural sphere is unimportant. As David Martin puts it:

> This dramatic restriction to the cultural sphere is, of course, one aspect of secularization, but whether this means that religion has finally ceased to be socially significant depends ... on whether culture is regarded as impotent and dependent. If culture is regarded as without serious influence then religion is indeed marginalized beyond recovery and can be dismissed as just one leisure-time activity among others (Martin, *ibid*).

It is at this point that the sociology of religion has much to gain from examining other contributions to the sociology of culture and ideology, particularly the interesting debates about 'postmodernism', ethnicity, nationalism, popular culture, legitimation, feminism, discourse, etc. (cf. Thompson, 1986). The common thread in all these debates is that culture is a relatively autonomous sphere of central importance for the reproduction of a social system, through processes such as the shaping of identity and subjectivity, legitimation of power and the winning of consent, regulation of bodies, and the disciplining and channelling of motivations and drives. In the classical theory of secularization, which equated it with institutional differentiation, the assumption was that religion surrendered its functions in these social processes to other institutions. This was believed to constitute grounds for accepting that religion was in decline. However, the fact that religion loses its monopoly position, need not mean that it declines. As the resurgence of market theory has taught us, competition can be good for organizations. It can sharpen them up, force them to identify consumer needs and to become more efficient in satisfying them. This no doubt applies to religious organizations, despite the difficulties they have in accepting utilitarian discourses and rationalities. (It may be easier for American churches because these elements are so pervasive in all institutional discourses and constitute a central feature of the national ideology).

The next question is: What are the market conditions in which religion may have a competitive advantage? Or, alternatively, in what circumstances does religion find itself in partnership with other institutions, and where does religious discourse syncretise with other discourses to gain in strength and importance?

The first question, concerning religion's 'market' position, has been answered in a number of ways. One view is that there is a 'supermarket of faiths' in Western societies which 'co-exist only because the wider society is so secular; because they are relatively unimportant consumer items' (Wilson 1975:80; see also Truzzi 1970, Fenn 1978). This view has been critized because it makes an assumption about the depth of commitment and authenticity of these religious groups compared with more traditional forms (Stark and Bainbridge 1985:437). A contrary hypothesis (cf. Stark and Bainbridge 1985), is that secularization itself stimulates religious revival in the form of movements, sects or cults, which are not trivial, particularly when they are innovative in their contents and supply what is lacking in those traditional religious organizations that have become internally secularized, in the sense of losing their distinctiveness from the surrounding world. The conclusion reached by Stark and Bainbridge is that:

> In the future, as in the past, religion will be shaped by secular forces but not destroyed. There will always be a need for gods and for the general compensators which only they can plausibly offer. Unless science transforms humans into gods or annihilates humanity, people will continue to live lives hemmed by limitations. So long as we exist, we shall yearn for a bounty of specific rewards, rewards that in the mundane world are too scarce to be shared by all, and we shall ache for those general rewards of peace, immortality, and boundless joy that have never been found this side of heaven. Secularization has unchained the human spirit, not stifled it in a rationalized bureaucratic outbox (Stark and Bainbridge 1985:527-8).

This positive conclusion about religion's prospects in relation to secularization, finds some echoes in David Martin's work. However, it is doubtful that David Martin would follow Stark and Bainbridge in their emphasis on religion as a source of compensations for relatively deprived individuals.

Essentially, this theory maintains that secularization weakens the capacity of traditional churches to offer distinctive compensations, because what they have to offer is relatively indistinguishable from that of the profane/mundane surrounding culture; consequently, sectarian schisms occur, based on a higher level of tension with the surrounding culture, but then their distinctiveness is gradually weakened by secularization. According to Stark and Bainbridge, cults which are distinguished by their cultural innovativeness (even if it is only new interpretations of old symbols), arise to fill the gaps left by the secularization or mundanization of established religious movements and faiths, and so cults are likely to go on proliferating.

Despite the attention given to the relationship of religion to the surrounding culture, this thesis still tends to concede that secularization pushes religion into the private sphere and is a matter of individual consumer choice of meaning systems to satisfy individual needs. In this respect it differs from most recent theories of culture, which ask how subjects - individuals or agents - are formed by culture. Similarly, the critique of secularization theories being offered here is that they too easily assume a continuing long-term decline of the potency of fundamental aspects of religious culture, such as the activity of the principles of symbolic community and the sacred as sources of identity. My own alternative thesis, based on a re-reading of Durkheim (Thompson 1990, 1986, 1982) is that the tensions produced by modernity stimulate assertions of total identity grounded in experiences of the socially-transcendent produced by symbolic community. The symbolic community is held to be of ultimate or sacred significance because it sustains a sense of total identity, as opposed to the partial roles and fragmented identities produced by the processes of rational-functional differentiation of modern social systems. For theoretical purposes, it does not matter whether the symbolic community is based on purely religious beliefs and practices, or whether it combines a mixture of discourses focused on the nation, sub-nation, ethnic group, or some other sub-culture or ideological cause. Communalization and sacralization are fundamental processes in all societies, whether or not we choose to use the term 'religion' in that connection. This conclusion may go beyond anything that David Martin has said, but I believe it is one of the possible theoretical implications to be drawn from his work, and it echoes Durkheim's conclusion:

> Thus there is something eternal in religion which is destined to survive all the particular symbols in which religious thought has successively enveloped itself. There can be no society which does not feel the need of upholding and reaffirming at regular intervals the collective sentiments and the collective ideas which make its unity and its personality (Durkheim 1965:474-5).

Bibliography

Durkheim, E 1965, *The Elementary Forms of the Religious Life*, New York: Free Press.

Fenn, R K 1978, *Toward a Theory of Secularization*, Ellington, Conn: Society for the Scientific Study of Religion.

Martin, D 1978, *A General Theory of Secularization*, Oxford: Blackwell.

Martin, D 1990, *Tongues of Fire: The Explosion of Protestantism in Latin America*, Oxford, Blackwell.

Stark, R and Bainbridge, W S 1985, *The Future of Religion: Secularization, Revival and Cult Formation*, Berkeley and Los Angeles: University of California Press.

Thompson, K 1970, *Bureaucracy and Church Reform: The Organizational Response of the Church of England to Social Change 1800-1965*, Oxford, Oxford University Press.

Thompson, K 1982, *Emile Durkheim*, London: Tavistock and Ellis Horwood.

Thompson, K 1986, *Beliefs and Ideology*, London: Tavistock and Ellis Horwood.

Thompson, K 1990, 'Secularization and Sacralization', in J.Alexander and P.Sztompka eds., *Rethinking Progress: Social Theory at the End of the Twentieth Century*, New York and London: Unwin Hyman.

Truzzi, M 1970, 'The Occult Revival as Popular Culture: Some Random Observations on the Old and Nouveau Witch', *Sociological Quarterly*, 13:16-36.

Wilson, B R 1975, 'The Secularization Debate', *Encounter* 45:77-83.

2
The Flowering and Deflowering of Protestantism in Latin America

Bryan Wilson

Macrocosmic sociology is a seductive, but by no means always a gratifying enterprise. The appeal of the summary overview of phenomena spanning diverse cultures or extended epochs is, ultimately, what we seek as the way of making sense of things. It is, none the less, an elusive goal. The greater the time-span or the space-span to be encompassed, so the more diverse the evidence, the harder to fit all the disparate pieces together, and the more tentative, and qualified the conclusions have to become. And this all the more so when some of those pieces are themselves highly specialised or localized studies of minutiae, altogether remote in scale from the scale of the final goal of a coherent and encompassing picture. To perceive the broad patterns, the secular trends, and the convergence and inter-relation of cultural, structural, economic and political processes, whilst keeping one's work free from gratuitous grand theoretical schemes, *a priori* assumptions, and abstract generalizations, is the tall order which the sociologist may set himself. It is, if I read him aright, just that tall order which David Martin has constantly had before him in his many-faceted scholarly output, and which in his latest work, is a goal which he surpassingly attains.

Tongues of Fire, the title of this most recent work, is a study of the expansion of Protestantism in contemporary Latin America (with some revealing comparative side-glances at Korea). It has all the commendable characteristics that we have long associated with Martin's work - breadth of vision, depth of scholarship, penetrating analysis, and the careful but never tedious presentation of appropriate supporting empirical material, constituting in all a distinguished addition to an already distinguished corpus. The successful methodological procedures adopted in the early work on *Pacifism* (1965), the adroit subsumption of a cluster of integral elements into type-constructs of a kind that Max Weber might have called 'historical individuals', is here employed again, as a way of making sense of, and of drawing into clearer perspective, diverse empirical evidence taken from a wide-ranging search of the growing body of literature - much of it the work of anthropologists - on aspects of religious change in Latin American culture. This material is vastly more diverse in quality and concerns, and applies to far more varied social situations, than did the empirical material that informed his 1967 book *A Sociology of English Religion*, but it is handled with the same characteristic sensitivity and attention to detail, and shows the same capacity to see beyond local case-studies to the wider explanatory cultural and historical realities.

The argument which this new book pursues, and in support of which the material is mobilized and the type-constructs marshalled, reveals, in type and substance, a close kinship with the cogent case made in *A General Theory of Secularization* (1978). That work was written in what I can only call a fugal mode - the steadily expanding outworking of a dominant thesis pursued from its bold statement in a first chapter outwards into varying ramifying implications - one might say, 'from centre to periphery'. So it is with *Tongues of Fire*. The *dramatis personae* of the typological narrative are not quite the same, but in a book in which history is extrapolated almost to prophecy, and which I am therefore tempted to call a 'foresight saga', the family resemblances are unmistakable.

The characters in *Tongues of Fire* are the successive generations of Protestantism - early Puritanism; succeeding Methodism; and eventual and recent and contemporary Pentecostalism, seen as three waves of influence; the first two spreading from Europe, and particularly from England, to America, with minor eddies affecting Latin America; and the third, a North American variant, now making deep inroads into what were once thought of as monolithically Catholic countries. These somewhat schematized currents of Protestantism and the residual Latin American Catholicism are seen as the religious influences of two contrasting cultural complexes - the Anglo-North American, and the Luso-Hispanic. Luso-Hispanic imperialism effloresces as militarism and male machismo: the Anglo-American is infused with Protestant virtues that represent peaceability, inner discipline, restraint - one might, indeed, say conscience, although Martin does not reduce these traits so baldly to that term which, none the less, is implicit in the argument.

Clearly these broad formulations demand - and receive - some modification in specific contexts, and the interaction of Protestantism and secular culture has produced its own distinctive accommodation in which 'conscience' has not always prevailed. Similarly, the place of the Roman Church vis-a-vis the state in the various Latin American republics with their diverse histories and economies, has not conformed to any one formula, as the secularist character of Uruguay, and the entrenched, indeed, retrenched place of Catholicism in Colombia, readily indicate. Such divergence is not only acknowledged, but is in large part explained in the pages of Martin's book. More than this: it is itself a focal point for a comparative analysis in respect of which the varying fortunes of evangelical religion can be appraised.

The Flowering of Pentecostalism

On his broad canvas, Martin treats of the purported underlying similarities not only among Latin American countries, but in defence of the ascription to culture - and more specifically of the ascription to religion - of the role of an independent variable in the historical process. The major instance that is cited, in which certain similarities are indicated, if not fully explored, is the Halévy thesis, which attributes to Methodism a significant part in preserving England from a revolution of the French type. That thesis, says Martin, provides the problematic for Pentecostalism in Latin America, implying, I infer, that without the contemporary expansion of Pentecostalism in Latin America, the energies now expended in consummatory religious activities might otherwise fuel the engine of social revolution. However, Latin America is a continent in which revolution has not been uncommon, and one may suggest that its diminishing incidence may be less attributable to the rise of Pentecostal religion than to the changes in social circumstances and in military technology which might render traditional popular revolution (the coup d'etat apart) no longer a viable recourse for discontented populations. Is late twentieth century Latin America sufficiently comparable to late eighteenth century England to make the analogy sustainable? And would those who have become Pentecostals actually be those who otherwise might man the barricades - if indeed, barricades are the relevant image for contemporary revolution?

What Martin shows is the *a*political disposition of the Protestants, at least of Evangelicals and Pentecostalists, who see things in dualistic terms of the Spirit against the World. And contempt for the world implies contempt above all for the politics and the powers of darkness. In Latin America, they find repellent both the atheistic doctrines of the Marxists and the secularists, and the Catholicism of many established parties. Martin sees the peaceable component in Anglo-Saxon Protestantism as persisting as a part of the inheritance even of Pentecostals. I do not doubt the possibility of this line of descent, but I wonder if this disposition is as strong in Pentecostalism as in some other Protestant sectarian movements. Where such an orientation occurs in Latin America, is it attributable to the inculcation of heightened conscience in response to specific doctrinal demands or is it a less conscious absorption of Protestant folk mores? Or is it perhaps the continuity of a certain political passivity amounting almost to fatalism which Martin acknowledges to be not uncharacteristic of the underclasses of Latin American societies? Only if it is rooted in a conscious orientation to the world and only if it displaces or transmutes real or potential aggressive dissidence might one firmly suppose that the Halévy thesis holds. The Pentecostals are generally a relatively unsophisticated public, not drawn, as Martin more than once points out, to the contemporarily available credo of Liberation Theology, which he declares to be merely an intellectual stance, not *of* the people so much as a middle class concern *for* the poor which is, however, alien to their local needs. With a safe, vigorous creed contending for their rights, and one that claims part of the Catholic tradition to which at least notionally they themselves once belonged, might not the poor, had they ever had revolutionary aspirations in mind, have chosen Liberation rather than Pentecost?

Their choice is very clear, however. The numerical impact of Pentecostalism is impressive. More then twenty years ago, it was estimated that some 15% of Chileans were Pentecostalists, and even a Roman Catholic authority acknowledged that there were on any given Sunday more people in Chile worshipping in Pentecostal communities than in Roman Catholic churches, and the movement has certainly advanced since then. Today it appears that in Brazil about 20% of the population is Protestant, the majority of them Pentecostals, and the number of full-time Protestant ministers, at 15,000, exceeds the number of Catholic priests, of whom there has always been a significant shortage in most Latin American countries, and many of whom were just as foreign to the indigenes as were the early Protestant missionaries from the United States. In Guatemala somewhere between 20% and 30% of the population are Protestants; in Nicaragua 20%; in Costa Rica 16%; in Mexico between 4% and 6%. What is almost certainly the case, too, is that those who count as Protestants are committed rather than purely nominal adherents, and everywhere there exists a penumbral further following, not yet counted as in membership: in contrast, Catholic figures notoriously embrace all the baptized, however nominal their allegiance may have become.

The advance of Protestantism on this frontier, represents as Martin sees it, a major breach in the generally hypothesized union of Church and State, faith and people. It represents the new availability of choice, and finds expression in lively worship, spontaneous faith, the spirit of participatory democracy (a contrast to the old hierarchic structure of religion) and in the realization of new bases of brotherhood. As Martin puts it, it introduces the ordered city of God to replace the confused city of man. Pentecostalism, and Protestantism more generally, is presented to us as a massive operation, no matter how randomly and at times chaotically organized, in consciousness raising.

Although it is not specifically invoked, the argument carried forward in respect to this phenomenon would fairly readily fit the relative deprivation thesis, but Martin is at pains to avoid an interpretation which ascribes to structural factors a determining role in the shaping of culture. He is committed from the first page to the view that understanding of the actors is vital to a sociological explanation of their activities - a view likely to find sympathy among British sociologists of religion, but not one always endorsed by those whose studies he has used in presenting his encompassing synthetic overview. Thus, we are told that it is the marginal people who are picked up by Protestantism, people who have, in one way or another, become detached or who have detached themselves from earlier ties and obligations, perhaps by becoming self-employed, or as small-holders, or by migration from the countryside to the new megacities.

Again, although there is no explicit discussion of the new faith in terms of functions, the actual functions of Protestantism, and thus at least in part its appeal, are frequently cited. It provides an indigenous expression of faith couched in the vernacular and accessible to ordinary men and women - the previously tongue-tied become inspirited. It provides networks and brotherhood, and thus emotional and often financial support. The new churches have become friendly societies, clubs, insurance agencies, and reorganized communities. They stand in sharp contrast to the frequent remoteness of the institutional Catholic church. They reinterpret values, confer identity, re-establish bonds, assert human equality and dignity, and at best they offer opportunity for the development of skills of expression and, in however rudimentary a way, organization.

The consequences of Protestantism in Latin America invite comparison with the Protestant ethic thesis in its classic locales. Martin notes indeed that Pentecostalism today is a far bigger phenomenon than Calvinism ever was: the implication appears to be that it is destined for perhaps an even more catalytic role in social development. He devotes a chapter to the economic implications of evangelical religion generally on this, the latest - perhaps the last? - frontier on which it now blossoms. There are, expectably, consequences to remark, but in this case are they in any sense as unintended as were the consequences of Calvinism? In some respects, converts perceive in advance the life-style and the economic benefits of the reformed system. They may observe that Protestants abandon the costly *fiesta* system with its ruinous demands on the poor, and the particularistic and probably corrupt institution of *compadres*, so long established in Catholic tradition. Evangelical Protestantism can be recognised as in some ways an exacting demand for a more rationalized and disciplined way of life, a life in which household budgeting, sustained work commitment, sobriety, thrift, honesty and punctuality are claimed to play a part, and in which male machismo has been relinquished. There is no mention of the impact of Protestantism on birth control which, one might suppose, might be of the greatest significance in the long run both for personal and familial well-being and the survival of Latin American societies. None the less, the various consequences to which Protestantism gives rise (the list I have chosen is explicitly indicated for the Mayas of Mexico) is indeed significant enough.

The question which arises, however, relates to the relationship between emotional religion and rationalized morality. It is evident that the austere and ascetic doctrines of Calvinism were of a piece with the moral dispositions which that faith inculcated: religion itself was sober; time was a conscientious concern, doctrinally prescribed; thrift was contingent on the rejection of hedonistic consumption; moral scruple and the searching of conscience were the direct correlates of the attainment of personal, individual autonomy. But Pentecostalism is not a vehicle of the same kind. Its doctrines were subordinate - at least in British and American Pentecostalism, and I should be surprised were this different in Latin America - to its practice, and its practice, especially in its early days, betrays a certain spiritual voluptuousness, not to say profligacy, which seems scarcely congruous with the moral asperity of the old Protestant ethic. Ecstasy - and Pentecostalism trades in ecstasy - is not so readily conjoined with rationality, and rationality was the underlying motif of the Calvinist ethic. Time is not a doctrinally enjoined conscientious concern in Pentecostal meetings, where services are often late to start and inclined to over-run.   Spiritual self-indulgence in tongue-speaking, in elaborate confession, testimonies of conversion and healing, and indulgent self-accusation, characterize Pentecostal practice, as I have seen it, in Europe and Africa.   Is individual autonomy so readily achieved in a body in which, as Martin repeatedly indicates, the network counts for so much and in which there is dependence on strong leadership which is a vital ingredient of the congregation's continued survival?   How well do these devotional orientations, and the style of organization, contribute to the archetypical virtues of classical Protestantism, which it may be said, are effectively carried - and in my experience more effectively carried - in the more rigorously organized sectarian movements of, for example, Seventh-day Adventists, Mormons, and Jehovah's Witnesses?

There is another different potential to the flowering of Pentecostalism in Latin America to which Martin alludes, namely the implication of voluntarism for societies, the central tradition of which, from the time of the Luso-Hispanic hegemony, has been the union of Church and State. At a societal level voluntarism intimates the likelihood that old Catholic parties must broaden their religious base, or abandon explicit claim to religious attachment if - once Pentecostal communities undergo a process of social re-accommodation - they are to draw the support of this growing section of the population.   More important, perhaps at the cultural level, the possibility of choice contains a latent threat to the cohesiveness of national culture; it creates channels of possible dissent; sets forth alternatives; confers the right to opt out of what are represented as national or societal concerns.   That some of those acquiring the right to opt out were, under earlier and less democratic regimes, often not consulted about being in, does not diminish the effect of what deliberate abstention and dissent might eventually effect.   For such a development not to be socially disruptive there must be a corollary: the privatization of faith must carry - as in its heyday in Europe the Protestant mainstream carried - the implication that protesting individuals are men of conscience, not merely choosing to 'think otherwise' and independently, but doing so with integrity and with some awareness of their moral obligation to the wider community. An ethic of responsibility was the guarantee that private choice would consult not only self-interest.   In Victorian England, that ethic was perhaps partially realized, but the Anglo-American experience indicates just how difficult it is to sustain in the long run such a decorous balance. Pentecostalism, like Methodism, was launched in a context of volatile emotionalism, but Pentecostalism lacks a Wesley, or any single leader of stature to exert authority.   It has evolved no effective organizational structure which can diffuse an enduring ethic of responsibility among those who pass through its portals, and who tomorrow, may pass beyond it, into a wider world of choice, as the prospects of more secular and perhaps more seductive indulgences than the purely spiritual are then opened up.

Prospects of Defloration

As yet in Latin America, Protestantism has not run far along the course that has characterised its development in Europe and North America. The Pentecostalists in Latin America remain - and perhaps all Latin American Protestants remain - more or less sectarian vis-a-vis the generally still entrenched Catholic Church, or, as in Guatemala, in relation to each other in a pluralistic situation in which fissile Protestant groups compete. As yet, there has been no effective process of denominationalization with its implications of mutual tolerance, and hence no incipient attenuation of commitment. This particular defloration of Protestantism has not yet occurred.

Protestantism has also shown a profound capacity to fragment - perhaps contingent on the open Bible, the emphasis on individual conscience and interpretation, and distrust of hierarchic authority. These are the seeds of its own decay, manifest also in the cultivation of critical detachment which is a solvent of absolute commitment. Protestantism, once ascendant, feeds on self-doubt and has everywhere a tendency to polarize. On the one hand is a liberal and Laodicean majority which merges into a larger or smaller constituency of indifferentists and tolerant unbelievers; and on the other hand, there persists a rump of sectarian fundamentalists. The process, which seems to be endemic in the Protestant position, is yet to get under way in Latin America, but with increasing literacy, the growth of an egalitarian ideology, and the abandonment of the still persisting remnants of the patron-client relationships inherited from traditional cultural patterns, there may yet be a worm in the bud.

These futuristic prospects go beyond the prophetic element in the discussion which Martin pursues, but there are other more immediately evident, if widely divergent, indications of the loss of innocence in Latin American Protestantism, and all of these receive some attention in this book. Since they amount to indictments of Protestantism on quite different counts, they must be treated separately as discrete issues. There is first the role of Protestantism as an agency of social disintegration particularly among tribal peoples. Although much more attention is paid to Protestant communities as agencies of re-integration of social and cultural values for dislocated individuals and families, the disruptive potential of the new faith cannot be ignored.

Obviously tribal cultures are under assault from other agencies beside Protestantism, some of them more compelling agencies than the mission, and as Martin comments, in one of his few barbed asides, the tribes cannot be kept in a condition of pristine innocence solely to meet the wishes of American anthropologists who need them as subject material for their Ph.D. theses. Yet Protestantism, particularly as it is purveyed by fundamentalist missionaries, is more immediately threatening, and in its own way more brutal than has typically been the case with the Catholic church. The spiritual division of labour sustained within Catholicism permits the laity

a certain latitude, not to say a laxity, whilst Protestants, and particularly
those of a fundamentalist persuasion - the persuasion most evident in Latin
America - inherit the idea of the priesthood of all believers, and even, at
times, the concept of every man a monk. They propound a moral rigour
and introduce patterns of intense socialization to absolute norms which
leave no cultural stone unturned. Folkways, customs, traditional
dispositions and indigenous social institutions all fall under the searchlight
scrutiny of the Protestant moral mentors.

Much tribal practice celebrates the turning points of the life cycle - birth,
puberty, courtship, marriage, conception and death - but these celebrations
almost invariably make explicit facets of life and human nature which
Protestants have spent centuries in repressing. Even the Pentecostals, who
are perhaps less intensely moralistic than are some other evangelical
groups, withdrew defeated from the settlements of the Toba Indians in
Argentina, when they discovered that what they had encouraged as
manifestations of the freedom of the Spirit by dancing, for the Toba carried
what the Pentecostals could not but see as lascivious intents. It is one
thing - and to Pentecostalists a disreputable thing - to dance out nature's
purposes and immediate human dispositions, and quite another, against the
centuries of restraint, repression, and cultivated repugnance for all directly
expressed sexual concerns, to manifest, albeit in physical expression not so
very dissimilar - the liberation of the spirit with claims (which not all
Protestants find convincing) to a more elevated source of spiritual joy.

Clearly, it is not easy for tribal peoples to perceive the subtle distinctions
of legitimation which encourage dancing and uttering tongues in the Spirit,
but interdict their own traditional ecstatic exercises. Might not the
similarity of forms indicate some ultimate similarity of function?
Pentecostals unleash patterns of action which gratify deep-seated instincts
which may have libidinal purposes, however much they are overlain - even
for these, the least sophisticated of Christians - with strong restraints.
Their ecstasies are interpreted as freedom licensed because they rest on
well-ingrained Christian discipline. Yet it is a commonplace that this
boundary is easily traversed: revivalistic practices have not infrequently run
from license to licentiousness. The Elmer Gantries are reincarnated as
Bakkers and Jimmy Swaggarts. The superficial similarities of expression
and perhaps the ultimate similarities of instinctual release may have given
this mode of Protestantism its immediate purchase in some instances, but
one may wonder, if the resocialization of illiterate and tribal peoples is
what is to happen, whether this form of Protestantism, whatever its
superficial appeal to its new clients, is the safest of vehicles.

A second sense in which Pentecostalism in Latin America (and not only
there) may be said to be less than virginal, is not unassociated with the
first. It is spiritually vulnerable to the locales in which it operates. The
mainstream of Protestantism, before its diversion into the ecstatic and
thaumaturgical concerns of Pentecostalism, militated vigorously, and
generally effectively, against all primitive forms of magic. Much more than

Catholicism, Protestantism refused to temporize with indigenous religion. Whether in the heartlands of Europe (where Pope Gregory the Great had once advised his missionaries not to interfere too much with the pre-Christian religion of the people), or in contemporary Brazil, where the Church does nothing to suppress the syncretistic African cults of Umbanda and the *Candombles*, Catholicism, even if draconian in its policies towards heresy, has often been lenient with paganism.

Although notionally Pentecostalism inherits the general Protestant orientation towards magical acts, it has none the less, opened the door to popular ecstatic revelation and has encouraged the belief in a god who frequently grants dispensations from normal causation in the matter of healing the body and in respect, at times, to other miraculous events. In Christianity generally, in respect for the supreme charisma of Christ, all subsequent claims to charismatic power have been in some measure muted, but in Pentecostalism there has been a democratization of charisma: all may become inspirited - indeed all *should* become inspirited. The demotic drift evident in Christian history (and in that of some other world religions) leads beyond the claim to the 'priesthood of all believers', and beyond the ideal of 'every man a monk', to that of every man, and even more emphatically, every woman, a prophet.

Given the ubiquity of spirits in local indigenous religions; the availability of magic; the frequency of oracles, and the expectation of miracles, it can be seen that Pentecostalism may enjoy an uneasy continuity with folk beliefs. Whilst contemporary liberal Protestantism could have little affinity with such traditional beliefs and practices, and the more austere fundamentalist sects and sections of Christianity would excoriate them entirely, Pentecostalism has an immediate proclivity for this nether-world of the spirits, even if re-interpreting it. For converts, traditional spirits can be re-categorized as the Holy Spirit or as the powers of darkness; glossolalia has continuities with traditional trance; magical curing can be assimilated to divine healing, which likewise may entail the laying on of hands and anointing. Just how fully and successfully such transmutations are effected, and just what residue of primeval belief remains doubtless varies from one locale to another, but Martin provides some indications. In Korea, which provides his comparative focus, he tells us of the amalgam of indigenous religion and conservative Protestantism: 'Shamanism and spiritism are nearly everywhere', he says. In Latin America, he refers to the 'substrata of almost universal spiritism', and he points to the magical elements in spiritual healing. He sees Pentecostalism, especially in its America missions, as combining the benefits of modern inventions, such as the encounter group and community medicine, with ageless, traditional healing techniques. All of it, of course, is done in the name of Protestantism. He notes that 'the long term resources now drawn upon in people's lives run back to the tradition of Protestant revival and to the ancient spirit worlds of Indian peasants and African slaves.' In an ecumenical age, such syncretism may even win applause, but it is a long way from what might be called the pristine Protestant vision.

The third evidence of the deflowering of Protestantism is of a different order. In the context of cultural imperialism, the religious mission may become a vehicle for national policy interests, or for economic interests of some within the missioning nation. Missions are a type of external patronage and patronage had been endemic in many parts of Latin America. Missionaries may knowingly serve or unwittingly represent the interests of their nation or its economy: they almost always carry the cultural assumptions of their home country. Martin is aware of the easy fusion of the image of American wealth and power with the explicit claims to be an avenue to power made in Pentecostalism. Powerless as most of its votaries are, the assertion that their faith confers power will become tangibly evident. Increase in wealth and social position is readily ascribed to God in Pentecostalism - it becomes proof in its own right, no matter what the ostensible attitude to material things may be. The prospect of increase of wealth and the acquisition of modern accoutrements through the mission stops short, no doubt, of being a slow-burning cargo cult, but the awareness of the disparity of circumstance between the recipient converts and beneficent missionaries and their American backers can scarcely be ignored.

Pentecostals in Latin America are frequently passive, world-rejecting communities, encapsulated in their own enclaves and generally apolitical. No military government nor even a shaky democracy - and scarcely without exception, Latin American governments are shaky - could ask for more than pliant, orderly, honest, conscientious citizens whose last concern is to meddle in political affairs or to campaign for political concessions. They may, as Martin indicates, at times become a silent pillar even for military dictatorships. At other times, the members of the new faith have been more active, and Martin notes the incidence of evangelicals in the Chilean Army (as indeed, they were in the special guard of the former dictator of Nicaragua), while their involvement in the government of Guatemala under General Rios Montt was more widely recognized, and may have been far from incidental. In some contexts, Protestantism may enter the lists as a vehicle for ideologies that are themselves far from spiritual.

There is, in the West, another potentially political facet of Pentecostalism which, although not dominant, should not entirely be ignored, even though Martin does not allude to it in this book. Certainly the primary orientation of the movement comprises conversion and charisma, thaumaturgy and ecstasy, but Pentecostals are also committed - as far as I know invariably - to belief in the second advent, and the reign of Christ as King. It may be that the advent is a waning as well as a waiting matter: imminence is not a quality for keeping, but I should be interested to know if this fundamental tenet of faith plays no part in Pentecostal affairs in Latin America, where people have more incentive to hope for such an event than have many of the relatively better-to-do Pentecostalists in the West.

Tongues of Fire finally turns to the question of secularization. Evangelical religion is restricted to the cultural sphere and this in itself, Martin concedes, may be said to be an indication of secularization, the loss by religion of its erstwhile presidency over social institutions. He ask whether this in fact means that religion has ceased to be socially significant. Is culture now impotent and dependent, marginalized and without serious consequences for the social structure? He sees two interpretations. First, Pentecostalism may be a temporary efflorescence like Methodism in England, accompanying a particular stage of industrialization and urbanization. Alternatively, there is a view, which regards the European experience as contingent and by no means the paradigm to which what takes place in other societies is likely or necessarily to approximate. The existence of a religious establishment in Europe inhibited the adaptability of religion to social change, and above all the industrial city. The North American paradigm, he believes, shows that once religion no longer entails relationship to a particular segment of the elite and to the state, then it might successfully adapt to a changing world, might become genuinely popular, inventive and successful in assuaging anomie.

No one, I think, would doubt the significance of specific historic and social structural circumstance in affecting the course of religious development. What occurs in one context certainly need be no model for what happens in another. The question is what influence religion might exert, where, and on what? Clearly, that must depend in part on its constituency: who are the carriers of the culture, and, within the culture, of what significance is religion's role? If the culture, as now manifest most visibly in the mass-media, is itself significantly secular in tone; if religion operates mainly in small and occasional face-to-face congregations, in contrast with the mass presentations of secular culture in television, radio, video, and the newspapers, then we might say that religion has ceased to command the cultural heights. Even in North America, where religion is certainly popular and inventive, it appears to be internally secularized and incapable of mobilizing either an effective political presence or restraint on the prevailing economic materialism. Such considerations must weigh even more when those who are recruited to the new faiths are themselves socially marginal, as appears to be the case in Latin America, living in what are described as segregated enclaves. Does not their social condition militate further against the exercise of much religious influence being exerted on the social structure, and even on the general culture? That religion will solace individual grief, provide a basis for social cohesion for some self-selected group, and serve as a protection against moral chaos, need not be doubted, but unless such groups move, as such, into the political and economic arena in a religious or religiously-inspired cause, will religion ever again affect in any significant way the operation of the social system?

The range of issues provoked by *Tongues of Fire*, of which only a sample has been alluded to here, marks it out as being more than merely a study of Latin American Protestantism, intrinsically important as that subject may also be. It is an exploration of the potential of religion in society - in polity and in economy as well as in morality, studied in a social context the volatility of which may still allow spiritual practices and their supporting ideology a role as an agency shaping human affairs. Just how much, in the process, Protestantism itself may be shaped and re-shaped is another, but an essentially contingent matter. What is apparent is that in watching the way in which these potentially powerful currents of thought and action work themselves out and influence, or are influenced by structural determinants, we now have the immense benefit of this widely researched and deeply thoughtful anticipatory investigation.

Bibliography

Martin, D 1965, *Pacifism*, London: Routledge and Kegan Paul.
Martin, D 1967, *A Sociology of English Religion*, London: Heinemann.
Martin, D 1978, *A General Theory of Secularization*, Oxford: Blackwell.
Martin, D 1990, *Tongues of Fire*, Oxford: Blackwell.

3
Cults for Capitalism
Self religions, Magic, and the Empowerment of Business

Paul Heelas

Curiously little attention has been paid by researchers to new religious movements and capitalist enterprise. Traditional Weberian concerns, to do with the meaning of work, specifically work ethics and motivation, do not deserve to be neglected. After all, most participants of most movements devote most of their daily time to economically productive activity. Although more is now being published on new religions and economic activity, most noticeably Richardson (1988), much remains to be explored.

One of the most significant expressions of 'new age' religiosity in the West treats the Self itself as the ultimate locus of Ultimacy or God. The organization known as 'est' is the most important of the self religions, as I call them, and during the last decade or so these movements have devoted increasing attention to the mainstream world of business. Accordingly, it has been asserted that self religions are fundamentally tarred by the brush of capitalism, indeed are not really religious at all. Are they basically to do with succeeding in the capitalist mainstream, or is priority attached to catering for spiritual concerns? The issue is highlighted by Marvin Harris, one of the most forceful and articulate proponents of the view that these movements serve utilitarian ends:

> In the more 'etherealized' and spiritualized 'trainings', the predominant, recurring theme is that of mind over matter. Not only do participants expect to control others by improving their control over themselves but they expect to control physical happenings by the imposition of their thoughts on matter. Erhard Seminars Training ('est'), for example, claims that thought is the basic stuff out of which the universe is constructed. Learning how to take responsibility for one's thoughts and to impose them on events therefore can lead to the kind of worldly success that est's founder, Werner Erhard, enjoys (1981:147).

More radical assertions are provided by Anthony Clare: 'All these cults are about nothing more than making money' (cited by Berman 1983:12). Claims that new religions are based on lies and deceit, utilizing slave labour to obtain money and power, are legion. The self religions certainly appear to offer this-worldly success, the magical powers which they unleash apparently being put to use with 'yuppie' ambitions in mind. Accordingly, it is easy to treat self religionists as capitalists, albeit in the guise of wierd magical utilitarianism.

My purpose is to undermine the claim that self religions show close affinities with the conventional world of business. Much hinges on the nature of magic. Does this practice differ from mainstream activities only by virtue of it being an unconventional technology (remaining conventional with regard to the ends aimed at), or is it bound up with a non-capitalistic vision of what is important about the market place? I argue that the first of these options does not do justice to the spiritual significance which participants attach to their activities and goals, and which ensures that magical technology should not be called into play in terms of attachment to utilitarian success. Attention to participant understanding - to which I attach great significance - reveals a very different picture of how the supra-market spiritual dynamic of the self religions, specifically the magical powers attributed to the Self, functions to empower work and obtain results in the capitalistic mainstream.

This claim must be qualified, for in the absence of adequate research it is impossible to say how many adepts of self religions seriously resist the temptation of becoming attached to mere worldly goals. Nevertheless, evidence from two movements - est and Exegesis/Programmes - reveals grave problems with the 'essentially capitalist' thesis, problems which also suggest that it canot be applied in cavalier fashion to the self religions as a whole. So far as I can tell, relatively detailed information about self religions, work and capitalism is limited to these two movements, the former studied by Steven Tipton, the latter by myself. Since Tipton's findings are readily available (1982a, 1982b, 1983, 1989) I largely draw on my research of Exegesis/Programmes, a London-based self religion-cum-business. Tipton's analysis, however, provides valuable support for the argument. Finally, the contention that the spiritual frame of reference must not be devalued should not be taken to imply that the argument has anything to do with ontological matters. Social scientists have to attend to what participants understand, not to the ultimate truth of their spiritual claims (cf. Thompson and Heelas 1986).

The self religions

First, a brief summary of the still relatively unfamiliar self religions (see Rhinehart 1976, Heelas 1982, 1985, 1987, 1990). est is taken as paradigmatic: it is the largest and most influential of movements which utilize 'processes', in the main drawn from the western psychotherapeutic tradition, to effect enlightenment, the experience of Self as God. Seminars introduce participants to themselves. The inspiration of American Werner Erhard, est is the transformational event (Erhard Seminars Training) which ran from 1971 (in London from 1977) until 'retired' in December 1984. During this period some half-million participated in the sixty hour or so 'educational' seminars, each paying, as of 1983, $400. According to an est publication, *The Network Review* (January 1985:2), 'another two million people have been introduced to transformation in workshops, special events, and seminars over the past 13 years'. Since the retirement of est, Erhard's path has continued, as The Forum for example.

The following self religions are among those directly influenced by est, in the main because their founders are est 'graduates'. They include Stewart Emery's Actualizations (Emery having been an est trainer) and John Hanley's Lifespring (Hanley was previously involved, with Erhard, in Alexander Everett's Mind Dynamics). These two movements had attracted some 200,000 people by as early as 1982. Then there is Robert D'Aubigny's London-based Exegesis (as well as being an est graduate, he tells me that he was influenced by Everett). Exegesis (1977-1984) attracted in excess of 6,000, each paying £200 plus VAT as of 1984. There is also est graduate Walter Bellin's Self Transformation (claiming 25,000 graduates in 1983), and John Roger's Insight (founded with the help of Russell Bishop, previously with Lifespring and with a claimed 100,000 participants). It is virtually certain that three million worldwide, probably four, have participated in the seminars of these and essentially similar movements since the early 1970's. Numbers swell if est precursors such as Scientology are included. Regarding the nature of self religiosity, Erhard and Gioscia write:

> In the [est] training, the experience of being at the effect of life - of having been put here, and having to suffer the circumstances of life, of being the bearer or victim of life, or at best, of succeeding or winning out over the burdens of life - *shifts* to an experience of originating life the *way* it is - creating your experience *as* you live it - in a space uniquely your own (1977:110).

The transformational 'shift' is from an unsatisfactory 'mechanical' way of living, where what we are by virtue of socialization (the 'ego' or 'mind') is in evidence, to a way of living which 'comes from' that which is as 'perfect' as perfection can be. As Erhard and Gioscia continue, in experiential mode,

> The experience of being yourself *is* innately satisfying. If who you really are does not give you the experience of health, happiness, love and full self-expression - or 'aliveness' - then that is not who you really are. When you experience yourself as yourself, that experience is innately satisfying. The experience of the self as the self *is* the experience of satisfaction. Nothing more, nothing less (*ibid*:111).

The experience of aliveness, it will be noted, is incompatible with attachment or commitment to the 'content' (beliefs, rules, jobs, etc.) of everyday, conventionally experienced, reality. Aliveness, or 'enlightenment', requires 'de-identification'. In the seminar, says Erhard, 'The person de-identifies with his mind, de-identifies with his body; he de-identifies with his emotions, he de-identifies with his problems, he de-identifies with his maya, he begins to see that he is not the Play' (1974:3).

Devil's advocacy

A satisfactory rebuttal of the claim that self religions are deeply imbued with the spirit of capitalism must face the facts, and indeed the essentially capitalist thesis is by no means implausible. Business activities are important, results matter, and magic is in evidence.

Business activities take three forms. Graduates band together to develop new enterprises, providing services (especially management and similar trainings) for companies in the mainstream; mainstream companies are 'converted' to self religiosity, members of such companies going to transformational seminars, returning to work, and encouraging others to take seminars; and self religions themselves operate as 'business' enterprises, with graduates running seminars and other activities. The Programmes group of companies provides an illustration of the first of these options, the great majority of the 180 workforce being Exegesis graduates. (Unless otherwise stated, material on Exegesis/Programmes pertains to the mid-1980's when I carried out research.) Most are employed by Programmes Ltd, a telephone marketing company which D'Aubigny helped to start in 1981; others work for Programmes Training Ltd, for example providing training in direct sales, communication, and management for mainstream companies such as IBM, Daihatsu and Whitbread; and a few work for a model and promotions agency, The Exhibitionists, or for Roar Music Limited. The Programmes group certainly looks like a mainstream, and successful, concern. Here is a business which a couple of years ago attracted the attention of the CBI, who saw 'enterprise' - not least because Programmes Ltd had rapidly expanded to become Europe's largest telephone marketing agency. Here is a business winning praise from other business-people and winning awards, for example the three top places of the British Direct Marketing Association's telephone marketing awards in 1984. Here is a business staffed by highly enthusiastic people working flat-out to obtain results, and indeed during my research at Programmes D'Aubigny told members that they had to stop working at 6.00 pm rather than carry on much later. As Jane McCarthy describes it, this is

> the most successful telephone marketing organisation in Britain at whose hub a group of young people of indomitable spirit has tackled the world of selling and emerged not only individually but also corporately truimphant.... Imagine a cross-fertilisation of the Stock Exchange plus the House of Commons and a bingo hall and you will have some idea of the Telephone Room (*Radio Times* 14-9-1983).

Other than Tipton's research which concentrates on est as a business, relatively little is known about est 'informed' enterprises - of which there are almost certainly many. Regarding one, Jeremy Main reports that 'Erhard's Transformational Technologies has licensed 58 small consulting firms for a fee of $20,000 plus 8% of the gross' (1988:78). He continues, 'They are selling his techniques to dozens of FORTUNE 500 companies'.

(According to Nicola Legat, in 1986 Transformational Technologies 'brought Erhard back $US15 million' - 1987:80). He also points out that although Transformational Technologies is run by est graduate James Selman, it is owned by Erhard (1988:86). The activities of one of the consulting firms is also described:

> David Spiwack, co-founder of one of the firms, IMW Consultants Inc. of New York, explains that his people tackle a company with a combination of workshops, interviews, and individual coaching of managers and engineers to help speed new product development, for example, he might work with a team of 25 executives for a year for a Fee of $25,000 plus expenses (1988:87).

The extent to which Erhard's organization operates in connection with the very heart of the capitalist mainstream can be gleaned from the fact that 'Clients of Transformational Technologies licensees include Allstate and Sears, General Dynamics, the Federal Aviation Administration, IBM, Boeing Aerospace, and Lockheed' (*ibid*). Another illustration is provided by a Licensed Affiliate of Transformational Technologies, employed to effect change among the workforce of a famous shipping company, including top management. Finally, here is an illustration of an (attempted) est inspired transformation of a mainstream company:

> Six former employees of the DeKalb Farmers Market in Atlanta, Ga., are suing their former employer, charging that they were fired or forced to resign because they refused to attend compulsory seminars.... The Forum, formerly known as est, directs its seminars at corporations. Early last year the owner of the DeKalb Farmers Market, Robert Blazer, attended a Forum seminar and began requiring nearly 500 employees to attend seminars.... Employees were forced to pay the $525 tuition through deductions from their paychecks (*Georgia Civil Liberties*, March 1988).

Neither should it be forgotten that est is a considerable 'business' in its own right. In the words of Tipton, it is a 'human potential' movement which from its beginnings has featured legal, financial and managerial structures drawn directly from the contemporary business world' (1988:223), and Rosen writes of 'the affinity between est and American business', the organization possessing 'a formidable top-down corporate structure' (1978:50). As early as the mid-1970's, est employed 230, helped by between 6,000 and 7,000 unpaid volunteers; writing of the early 1980's, Tipton reports that this 'model bureaucracy' has 300 paid employees and 25,000 volunteers, and that 'est grossed some $30 million in 1981' (1982b:190; 1988:224).

More support for the essentially capitalistic thesis is provided by the role played by magic. Graduates of the self religions frequently hold that the Self itself has power, in the sense that what happens in the world - and not simply experience of it - is Self-dependent and can transgress scientific understanding of causality. Thus members of Exegesis/Programmes hold that when one is 'at cause', or living in terms of the 'source' that is the Self itself, as opposed to 'at effect', or living in terms of the mind, events naturally fall into 'alignmment' with the perfection that is the Self. When one is at source, one does not fear illness - as smokers liked to tell me! One is not late: excuses provided by Exegesis seminar participants who arrived after sessions began were not accepted; it was their responsiblity that the tube had broken down or whatever. One does not have accidents: was one informant joking when she claimed to be able to cross a busy road without looking? The magical outlook informs Programmes Managing Director Elisabeth Gluck's observation, reported in the *Radio Times* (September 1983), 'It doesn't ever occur to anyone here to be ill or late'. As for the role played by the power of the Self to obtain business results, consider the following dialogue, which begins with a tele-sales person explaining her lack of success - 'Between three and four I had a lot of problems with engaged signals' - and continues,

> TEAM LEADER : Your comment about the engaged tones, I don't want to hear it. If someone comes to you and says, "I've got a lot of engaged tones", would you say to them, "Ah, never mind", or would you say "Take a look at your energy, and the amount of intention you're putting out"?
> PHONERS : The energy, the intention.
> LEADER : You know the dynamics of getting through and you know how to get orders. It's *simply* putting our energy, and being consistent with your intentions. You fell asleep for an hour. It's about energy and consistency, isn't it?
> PHONERS : Yes!
> LEADER : Then get it! ('The Second Oldest Profession', BBC1, Sept 1983).

Or as Gluck told me, 'When the phone is engaged, you are not in'.
est is just as magical, a vivid illustration being provided by a trainer who tells seminar participants, 'I can exert my consciousness into the mineral, animal, human and cosmic realms, at any time, on any planet, in any galaxy, anywhere in the universe' (Garvey 1980). As Tipton states, 'the individual's inner state determines his external achievement which in turn mirrors it' (1982b:201). He provides examples of magic in the workplace. A former employee of a franchise operation run according to est principles, and who had been engaged in door to door selling, says, 'if no one was home, it was because you weren't home' (*ibid*). In line with telephoning at Programmes, Tipton also reports an est staff member saying, 'there I sat, dialing the telephone, hour after hour - nobody home ... Finally, I realized that it was me who wasn't "home"' (1982a:214).

More evidence to support the essentially capitalistic thesis is provided by the fact that self religions appear to promise greater success, and imply, or explicitly state, that this includes business endeavour. An Exegesis brochure 'The Exegesis Programme' asserts that the seminar serves 'to release amd direct their [participants'] energy towards any chosen goal'. Zemke writes that Erhard has 'aimed' The Forum 'at the corporate market' (1987:26), and indeed the 1988 brochure refers to 'the magic of The

Forum', a magic of *'being* itself' which 'promises to produce an extraordinary advantage in your personal effectiveness and a decisive edge in you ability to achieve'. Erhard proclaims, 'The organizing principle of est is: Whatever the world is doing, get it to do that' (cited by Bartley 1978:221). Tipton reports of est, 'If the individual has realized his true inner self ... he can achieve and gain whatever he wants' (1982a:211). There are also organizations and seminars with names like Results Unlimited or Creating Success. With this kind of presentation, it is not surprising that mainstream businesses often judge them to have commercial utility, and invest accordingly. Self religionists, it appears, make good capitalists (cf. Rosen's claim that 'many businesses say they "prefer" est graduates in their job ads' (1978:50); cf. Legat 1987:80).

Another consideration is that self religions frequently attract people who might be expected to be seeking ways to become yet more successful in the mainstream, such as Ken Wilber's 'new age yuppies' who 'are the '60s mentality grown up and in the marketplace, where they continue to "want it all"' (1987:11; cf. Wallis 1984:28-9). Life-style expectations would lend prima facie support to the claim that magic, once experienced during seminars, is utilized in utilitarian fashion; is employed to become more successful in the fast lane. Thus during the 1980s self religions have tended to recruit consumeristically-minded people, more attached to the mainstream than their predecessors who were often hankering after expressive values (on this last point see Tipton 1982a:180-186; 1982b:191-2; 1983:272). It is true that the 'affluent and successful looking' people in their 30s and 40s, including 'the city's smart set of designers, people from the fashion world, theatre people, and the media' whom Legat saw at The Forum in Auckland (1987:63), might well adopt The Forum's message that *attachment* to success in their careers is not the way to live. But in the longer term these peoples' career attachments might well come back to prominence. If indeed they have experienced their power, it is to be expected that some will employ magic to empower their competitive activities.

Study of Exegesis and Programmes provides some support. Over half the 50 participating in the seminar observed in 1984 were business-people, calling to mind Legat's observation that 'most of the 2000 people Werner Erhard addressed in Sydney last year were from the business community' (1987:80). A follow-up questionnaire, four months later, suggests that some graduates might be utilizing their newly realized powers to fulfill their worldly ambitions, and according to the judgement of people working at Programmes, a number of graduates working for other companies, including two predominantly staffed by Exegites, employ magic in utilitarian mode.

The essentially capitalist thesis can be buttressed further. Some might find it significant that 'Werner is proud of his business background and credits it with being an important factor both in his enlightenment and as the school in which he learned much of what preceded est' (Bry 1977:114).

Bry continues by citing Erhard on how he introduced Zen - a significant influence on est - to business, and what this has to do with getting results:

> One place you are really allowed to do things like this [applying spiritual disciplines] is business, because business doesn't care what you do as long as it isn't illegal and produces results. So when I told the boss I was going to use Zen with the sales force, he said, "Great, don't get any on the walls". So I got a chance to take my experience in Zen and translate it from the usual setting to a new setting ... The thing that was really beautiful about this translation of disciplines into business - you really had to find out what the hell was trappings and drop it fast.

The implication is that Zen, without 'trappings', is what gets sales, and it appears that sales matter.

The nature and role of magic and the empowerment of capitalism

It would be rash to rule out the possibility that a fair number of self religionists operate as magical utilitarians, relishing their understanding of self religiosity which defines the nature of power in terms of market utility. However, there is strong evidence of self religionists who might be 'capitalists' in that they work 'within' the system and aspire to 'achieve' accordingly, but who are not capitalists in that they are not committed to capitalism per se. Considering this in connection with Programmes, the key to the matter is that participants say they are engaged in, or have to varying degrees effected, 'the transformation of business', a transformation which is bound up with the application and cultivation of Exegetical spirituality in the business milieu. The meaning of work - what members work for (their work ethic) and how they understand the dynamics of work (including the nature and role of magic) - must be understood in terms of this context. Success and how to obtain it is defined in terms of spiritual-cum-'capitalistic' dynamics, values and, ultimately, ontology.

The transformation of business means that business activities are taken to provide the opportunity to 'work' on oneself in a learning environment, 'a context where seminar principles are operative' as D'Aubigny told me. They help participants discover and experience what is ultimately valued, the God within. This is what D'Aubigny has in mind when he talks about 'how to make an organization serve the real needs of an individual' ('Newsnight', BBC1, 1983). The same is intended by Kim Coe, another key figure, when she says in the same programme

> The idea, the principle that we run on and that this organization depends upon, is the fact that the only thing that satisfies is the experience and challenge of personal growth. If you are here simply to have a job, you will find the situation very uncomfortable. This is a growing, learning environment ... (cf. Erhard, cited by Tipton 1983:276).

Now business can only operate as a learning environment if participants are not attached to conventional business activity. Such attachment to the World of Mammon merely encourages ego-operations, thereby erecting barriers to Self-actualization. Since participants are operating within the capitalist system, how is it possible to claim to be detached? The answer is that although the 'content' of mainstream business, or the nuts and bolts operations and tasks of capitalist enterprise, remains more or less unchanged, it has to be experienced from a 'context' - the Self - which rules out attachment. (For more on est's virtually identical formulation, see Erhard and Gioscia 1977:112, Tipton 1982b:198, and the est brochure 'Questions People Ask about the est Training'). Finally by way of introduction, the work ethic of transformed business life, what I call the monistic self-work ethic, empowers the business-place. Self religionists at Programmes work hard, indeed extremely hard at tele-sales and other tasks, but not in terms of a utilitarian ethic with all its materialistic attachments. The main justification for effort is that work is treated as a significant means to the end of Self-actualization.

In a nutshell, the transformation of business is held to cater for the ultimate value of Self-actualization by enabling participants to work on themselves whilst working productively for the group of companies, but without letting the content of capitalism and associated ego-operations come into dominance.

Substantial evidence shows that Self-actualization is of ultimate value at Programmes. A questionnaire, answered by virtually all the workforce, shows three-quarters to be quite explicit about their self religiosity. One reply - 'I believe in a God but through me, I am my own God' - is typical. Conversational interviews show that the great majority are only too keen to emphasise the importance of their monistic quest. Then there is the consideration that almost all at Programmes could be earning much more elsewhere, and by doing jobs which conventional wisdom holds to be more challenging and exciting. This well-educated workforce, many of whom had previously been successful in the mainstream, is certainly over-qualified for tele-sales and would not be engaged in the task of selling over the phone if priority was attached to conventional career aspirations. For if this were so they would surely find more lucrative jobs, let alone jobs which are more challenging than the dire task of telephoning for hour after hour. Phoners at Programmes, it can be noted, are paid the going rate for the job, but significantly enough are not paid on a bonus format.

The claim that the primary reason people work at Programmes is because they are on a spiritual not a capitalistic quest, experiencing their work as being about a transformational dimension which transcends mere profit maximization, is supported by another line of inquiry. Use of a psychological assessment questionnaire, the California Psychological Inventory, shows that 80% of the workforce, rather than the 40% of the control sample, are 'gamma' personalities. According to CPI literature provided by Burt McHenry, the psychologist who has helped with this analysis,

> Gammas are the doubters, the skeptics, those who see and resist the imperfections and arbitrary limits of the status quo. At their best, they are innovative and insightful creators of new ideas, new products, and new social forms; at their worst, they are merely rebellious, recalcitrant, and disruptive.

And gammas at Programmes tend to be located towards the 'worst' end of this spectrum. These are not the kind of people one would expect to find accepting the discipline and tedium of tele-sales. McHenry exclaimed on first seeing the CPI results, 'Programmes cannot work!' That it does, and so successfully, provides very strong evidence that participants are finding out-of-the-ordinary value in their work, and the obvious candidate is that work is valued as a means to a spiritual end. Additional support for this is provided by all those who state that tele-sales per se is not the point. Nick Vesey, a leading figure, says on the TV programme 'The Second Oldest Profession' that 'none of us are particularly fascinated with telephone marketing, and none of us are particularly fascinated with selling'. As Coe told me, 'phoning is not the issue; the people phoning are'. These are not the observations of people attached to their jobs; these are the observations of people who aim to be detached from their work whilst working on themselves. (See also Tipton 1982b, Bird and Westley 1988:59-60).

Having established the meaning of work at Programmes, how does it bear on the nature of magic and its role in the empowerment of 'capitalism'? As should be apparent, the transformational context means that participants should not tap their powers as a short cut to obtain goals intrinsically valued in terms of the capitalist nexus. And indeed since it is impossible to be at cause when cathected to the mainstream, magic employed for utilitarian purposes cannot work. Participants who so to speak commodify their magical powers are criticised for being 'on it'. And so to the crux of the matter - the role which is left for magic. What has been said does not rule out magic being valued as a means to the end of 'capitalistic' success. Financial rewards of work-cum-magic are important, not least because it is fully acknowledged that Programmes requires income in order to prosper and pursue its goal of transforming society as a whole (see Heelas 1987:21; cf. 1985). But since the most significant goal is Self-sacralization, this provides the primary context for understanding magic. Thus the experience of magical efficacy has an important role to play in how telephoning, and other activities, serve as spiritual disciplines. Since sales results reflect one's state of being - failure to obtain them is a sign of 'being at effect', success of 'being at cause' - phoning enables workers to 'test the hold of the ego'. They can monitor their spiritual progress. And someone is always available to apply seminar-like 'processes' to those who have lapsed to being at effect or 'on it', attached to their role and personality. In addition to signalling the need for action, telephoning itself provides an opportunity to practice being at cause. Phoners treat their work as a means to the end of Self-actualization because it provides them with the opportunity to 'push through their resistance, the barriers that come up, their experience of being at effect', as one person put it. In the transformed world of Programmes, talk is of 'Zen and the art of telephoning'. This technique of transformation is the self-work ethic put into practice. In a manner of speaking, one phones oneself 'up'. As Coe says, 'We are using the phone to create greater power within ourselves'. 'Goal setting' and achievement, of great importance at Programmes, serves to 'throw into relief the experience of being at source'. est, it can be noted, appears to attach equal if not more importance to the view that achieving results is a transformed experience: 'According to est's ethic, the individual's felt well-being ['aliveness'] follows from his having a life that works, which follows from his setting goals and achieving them' (Tipton 1982a:211).

All this has profound consequences for what it is that empowers 'capitalism' at Programmes. The outside observer is unlikely to agree with participants that magic itself can obtain results. The more likely story is that the monistic self-work ethic plays an important role in instilling an ethos conducive to hard work. Empowerment is a matter of motivation. The main reason why such an unlikely workforce is hard at work selling over the phone, for less pay than they could readily be receiving elsewhere, is that work is part of the 'seminar' that is Programmes. Through work participants work on themselves, and it is valued because it is a means to this ultimate end. And people work hard in order to obtain what matters to them. Furthermore, although 'capitalistic' results are basically valued because they provide a sign of being at cause, a mark of success, however temporary, in the quest for Self-sacralization, the workforce is also motivated to produce the goods necessary for expansion and the transformation of society at large. Finally, it should be pointed out that the outside observer, especially if social psychologically-minded, might draw attention to aspects of the motivational process which participants would not be so happy to see attributed to the monistic self-work ethic. Thus it can be claimed that participants work hard because they are afraid of losing face and position in the spiritual hierarchy. Self religiosity radicalizes 'responsibility', an important term at Programmes, in that the Self is ultimately responsible for results. Since failure to get business results publicly demonstrates spiritual failure, people strive to be successful.

Conclusion

Efforts have been directed to revealing the reductionistic nature of the essentially capitalist thesis. The heart of the matter lies with the participant-based claim that capitalism is transformed. Utilitarian values and goals, in terms of which one works for oneself, satisfying one's desire for material rewards and not significantly changing in the process, give way to spiritual values, in terms of which one works on oneself according to the dynamics of Self-sacralization. The secret lies in finding oneself through 'work', the transformational teaching ruling out attachment to commercial success as that is normally understood, together with any attempts to employ magic accordingly. As for how 'capitalism' is empowered, the monistic self-work ethic - where magic has a central role at Programmes - means that endeavours to obtain results are part-and-parcel of the quest for what is of Ultimate value. This explains why an improbable workforce is so highly motivated whilst telephoning, and without mere reliance on the value of individual wealth accumulation. This explains why a work environment which one might expect to be alienating and repressive, a veritable 'iron cage', is taken to be in alignment with spiritual concerns, indeed, is experienced as enlightening. (Cf. Tipton's interpretation: 'For committed est graduates, the meaning of mundane work has been redeemed as a means to the sacred end of "expanding your aliveness"' - 1982b:203). Looking further afield, I strongly suspect that this non-reductionist account provides a more satisfactory portrayal of the self religions than that of dedicated capitalism. It is especially significant that those at Programmes, deeply immersed in magicality and obtaining results, nevertheless know that magic cannot be employed in terms of mere career attachment or worldly ambition.

What needs to be emphasised is how transformed business bears on what counts as success, namely that work is valued as a means to *both* spiritual and 'capitalistic' ends. Unlike those eastern traditions which only focus on the search within, the fact that the latter is an aspect of the perfection of being 'at cause', means that they can have the the best of both worlds. The inner search is all that matters, but since 'worldly' success is a spiritually significant 'goal' the search incorporates prosperity in the market place. And although participants might not be committed to making money, they have the power to make plenty of it. Erhard is a rich man. However, he says, 'I've worked on becoming a millionaire and I'm totally clear on how much bullshit that is. Where I'm at with money is that I'm not attached to it' (quoted by Bry 1977:117). 'Money', as he puts it, is 'no substitute for satisfaction'(1977:112); 'the value people experience in est cannot be measured in money' (quoted by Tipton 1988:237). However, the fact remains Erhard teaches that success results when attachment to capitalistic goals is 'devalued', that is, treated in terms of the Self itself: 'When [conventionally envisaged] success was no longer his highest goal - when he had been converted from it - he began to succeed in all his business activities' (Bartley 1978:138). Whatever the reader might make of this way of incorporating, whilst transforming, material goals, such teachings must be taken seriously in the portrayal and analysis of how participants understand self religiosity. For many, what might have first seemed to be a religion for yuppies transpires to involve something else. They shift from affirming the mainstream to experiencing it (not least its benefits) in terms of their transformational path (cf. Heelas 1985 for a critique of Wallis's (1984) category of 'world-affirming' movements).

Analysis of the theology of enlightenment and prosperity advocated by Programmes and est prompts reflection on a number of additional matters, all deserving further inquiry (cf. Heelas, forthcoming). First, there is the question of whether people are attracted to the self religions because they are seeking materialistic advantage or because they are reacting to western materialism whilst searching for eastern-inspired spirituality (cf. Harris 1981). My portrayal largely has to do with how participants, not those attracted, understand self religiosity. However, reference has been made to self religions attracting many from the world of business, in measure presenting themselves as ways of improving business efficacy (for qualifications on Exegesis see Heelas 1987). Second, there are a number of interesting questions to do with the transformation of business-cum-work ethics, including how such endeavours compare with those found in somewhat more humanistic forms of self-actualization. (see for example Adams (ed) 1984, 1986, Evans and Russell 1989, Ferguson 1981, Ray and Myers 1986, Reich 1971, Roszak 1981 and Yankelovich 1983).

More research is also needed to establish whether attempts to transform business, so that self religionists can operate 'in' the world of capitalism without ego operations coming to the fore, is a stable or precarious endeavour. This issue has commercial implications. Members of transformed businesses work hard to detach themselves from ego-operations. Spirituality should flourish 'in' the mainstream, and to the extent that it does the work ethic is of a monistic variety. This contributes to high levels of motivation, and so to the ability of movements to obtain those resources required to finance their world transforming activities. 'Capitalist' enterprise and movement resource mobilization is de-empowered if what prevents secularization of the workplace, namely the experience of transformation, is eroded by attachment to materialistic values and greed. And indeed, since my research in the mid-1980's it appears that Programmes has become a more conventional, albeit still magically-minded, enterprise. It seems that talk today is more of 'satisfaction' than self as God.

Finally, questions are raised by the practice of magic. The last few decades have witnessed a resurgence of magicality in the west. To what extent do those many new age paths which teach the unlimited power of the Self differ from est-like self movements with regard to how magic is employed in connection with spirituality and prosperity? (see Adler 1986 and articles in the *New Age Journal* on new age magicality). The role played by magic in the est-like movements can also be compared with those humanistic and human potential management trainings which advocate psychologized versions of something akin to magic; or with the 'positive thinking' and 'mind science' traditions, fundamentalistic 'prosperity theology', 'thelemic magick' (Melton 1983), and witchcraft movements (cf. Luhrmann 1989). Tanya Luhrmann's account serves to raise an interesting comparative issue, for unlike self religionists her informants only rarely suggest that they use magic in business (1989:8). Then there is the question, 'Why is magic practised when, according to the researcher, it does not work'? The self religions manifest the intrusion of magic in the heartland of rationalized and technologified modernity. Anthropological theories might help explain this (cf. Luhrmann 1989), although more psychological approaches are probably most useful in explaining how transformational seminars encourage participants to experience what they consider to be their magicality.

Bibliography

Adams, J (ed) 1984 *Transforming Work*, Virginia: Miles River Press.

Adams, J (ed) 1986 *Transforming Leadership*, Virginia: Miles River Press.

Adler, M 1986 *Drawing Down the Moon*, Boston: Beacon.

Bartley, W 1978 *Werner Erhard*, New York: Clarkson N. Potter.

Berman, C 1983 'Cults for Capitalism', *New Statesman,* 8th April: 11-12.

Bird, F and Wesley, F 1988 'The Economic Strategies of the New Religious Movements', in Richardson, J (ed) *Money and Power in the New Religions*, Lampeter: The Edwin Mellen Press, pp.45-68.

Bry, A 1977 *est*, London: Turnstone.

Erhard, W 1974 'Werner Erhard: All I can Do is Lie', (interview) *East West Journal* (Sept.).

Erhard, W and Gioscia, V 1977 'The est Standard Training', *Biosci. Commun.*, 3: 104-122.

Evans, R and Russell, P 1989 *The Creative Manager*, London: Unwin Hyman.

Ferguson, M 1981 *The Aquarian Conspiracy*, London: Routledge & Kegan Paul.

Garvey, K 1980 'An est Experience', *Our Town*, 10/15, March 2nd-8th.

Harris, M 1981 *America Now*, New York: Simon & Schuster.

Heelas, P 1982 'Californian Self Religions and Socializing the Subjective', in Barker, E (ed) *New Religious Movements: A Perspective for Understanding Society*, New York: The Edwin Mellen Press, pp.69-85.

Heelas, P 1985 'New Religious Movements in Perspective', *Religion*, 15: 81-97.

Heelas, P 1987 'Exegesis: Methods and Aims', in Peter Clarke (ed) *The New Evangelists. Recruitment, Methods and Aims of New Religious Movements*, London: Ethnographica, pp.17-41.

Heelas, P 1990 'The Economics of New Religious Life', *Religion*, 20: 297-302.

Heelas, P (forthcoming) 'The Sacralization of the Self and New Age Capitalism', in Abercrombie, N and Warde, A (eds) *Social Change in Contemporary Britain*, Cambridge: Polity Press.

Legat, N 1987 'Formers: The New Navel-Gazers', *Metro*, (Oct.): 60-80.

Luhrmann, T 1989 *Persuasions of the Witch's Craft*, Oxford: Blackwell.

Main, Jeremy 1988 'Trying to Bend Manager's Minds', *Fortune International*, (Nov 23rd) 25: 77-90.

Melton. G 1983 'Thelemic Magick in America', in Fichte, J (ed) *Alternatives to American Mainline Churches*, New York: Rose of Sharon Press, pp.67-87.

Ray, M and Myers, R 1986 *Creativity in Business*, New York: Doubleday.

Reich, C 1971 *The Greening of America*, Harmondsworth: Penguin.

Rhinehart, L 1976 *The Book of est*, New York: Holt, Rinehart & Winston.

Richardson, J (ed) 1988 *Money and Power in the New Religions*, Lampeter: The Edwin Mellen Press.

Rosen, R 1978 *Psychobabble*, London: Wildwood House.

Roszak, T 1981 *Person/Planet*, London: Granada.

Tipton, S 1982a *Getting Saved from the Sixties*, London: University of California Press.

Tipton, S 1982b 'The Moral Logic of Alternative Religions', *Daedalus*, (Winter): 185-213.

Tipton, S 1983 'Making the World Work : Ideas of Social Responsibility in the "Human Potential movement"', in Barker, E (ed) *Of Gods and Men*, Macon: Mercer Press.

Tipton, S 1988 'Rationalizing Religion as a Corporate Enterprise: The Case of est', in Richardson, J (ed) 1988: 223-240.

Thompson, J and Heelas, P 1986 *The Way of the Heart: The Rajneesh Movement*, Wellingborough: The Aquarian Press.

Wallis, R 1984 *The Elementary Forms of the New Religious Life*, London: Routledge & Kegan Paul.

Wilber, K. 1987 'Baby-Boomers, Narcissism, and the New Age', *Vajradhatu Sun*, 9/1 (Oct/Nov): 11-12.

Yankelovich, D et al 1983 *Work and Human Values*, New York: Aspen Institute for Humanistic Studies.

Zemke, R 1987 'What's New in the New Age?' *Training*, (Sept): 25-33.

4
Faith, Charity and the Free Market

Anne Eyre

This chapter is about the impact of the 'enterprise culture', emphasising freedom, personal responsibility and the family, currently being fostered by Britain's Conservative government, on welfare provision, changing perceptions of social need and the role of the charity sector. The traditional role of the churches in charitable relief has largely been taken over by the state, but contemporary government policy is attempting to reverse this trend. The primary objective of Conservative social policy is to reduce people's dependence on the state, and this is to be achieved by cutting expenditure on social welfare and replacing universally-provided benefits with a 'cash-limited' Social Fund. Ethical legitimation for these policies is given by the 'trickle-down theory', in which it is maintained that tax cuts and other incentives will lead to the generation of new wealth, a share of which individuals and businesses will be more inclined to give to charitable causes. Charitable bodies will increasingly become the main providers of welfare. But will this stand up to empirical testing? Will people become more generous as the needy come to depend increasingly on them? What are the ideological implications of shifting the burden of responsibility for welfare away from the state onto individual and corporate philanthropy?

The 'trickle-down theory'

Underpinning the British Conservative government's economic and social policies is the conviction that the state's help to the poor should be confined to a 'safety net' to catch the poorest. The belief is that the poor can be helped towards prosperity only by making the nation wealthier. The creation of new wealth, it is suggested, follows from policies including cutting public expenditure, lowering taxation and deregulating the economy. As the rich create more wealth, some of this will, in time, trickle down to the poor. In 1987 the Director General of the Institute of Directors said 'The best way for capitalism to care is to succeed'. These policies promote a system of inequality. It is believed that those at the top have the best incentive to work, to invest, to take risks and succeed. This emphasis on the achievers in the system has been reflected in recent government welfare changes.

Government welfare changes

Among a number of benefit changes introduced by the government in April 1988 was a change in arrangements for emergency support from the previous system of 'one-off' single grant payments to a system of loans from a 'Social Fund'. Each local office of the Department of Social Security now has a fixed budget from which loans are made for essentials such as furniture, cookers etc. The essence of the policy is that no one any longer has a legal right to emergency help; decisions are discretionary and not subject to independent appeal. The emphasis is on loans, not grants. The aim of these social security changes is to decrease dependence on the state and increase the role of charities so that they will work in partnership with the DSS. Managers of the Social Fund are expected to advise claimants to appeal to charities if the Fund cannot meet their needs. As the then Home Secretary Douglas Hurd put it:

> In education and in housing, as well as in crime prevention, private enterprise and the charitable sector can often meet particular local needs and local difficulties in a way that the bureaucratic and inflexible agencies of either central or local government find impossible (*Church Times*,4/9/88).

Various tax changes have been made to encourage the public to give more generously to charitable causes. In the 1988 Budget the Chancellor of the Exchequer made tax cuts amounting to £6 billion. Of this, £1.9 billion went to the top 1% of all taxpayers with incomes over £50,000. By comparison the 12% of all taxpayers with incomes under £5,000 gained only £120 million. In 1987 he had introduced a 'Give As You Earn' scheme allowing employees to give up to £120 a year tax-free through pay-packet deductions. As a result of these changes, it was estimated that charities would benefit to the tune of £100 million in new donations, but in the first nine months the scheme only generated half a million pounds.

British charitable giving

Is the British public becoming more generous? The picture is a complex one. Some figures indicate that charitable giving has more than doubled in the last ten years and that giving by both individuals and companies is going up. But there is little evidence to suggest that those who benefited from the 1988 tax cuts are giving more generously. Less than 3% of those interviewed in a survey published in *The Guardian* in October 1988 said that they were now giving more to charity. So which groups are giving more? And what proportion of increased company profits is being given to charity and what is the motivation behind giving? Clearly some charities have benefited more than others from the rise in donations.

It is estimated that £10 billion a year is given to the 18,000 registered charities in Britain. Of these, the ones doing best are the Save the Children Fund, the National Society for the Prevention of Cruelty to Children and Oxfam, with the religious aid societies coming next.

The mass media have had a significant impact on the fund raising. The Children In Need Appeal was first introduced in 1927, but since the television presenter Terry Wogan raised £1 million on television in 1980 it has become an annual appeal broadcast on television and radio. In 1988 it raised £17.5 million (of which £8 million was pledged on the night).

In the same year Britain's commercial television network mounted its first 'Telethon' with £21 million pledged on air.

These figures can be compared with the Catholic Fund for Overseas Development's annual income of £11 million, of which £3 million comes from government grants. The Church Urban Fund the charity set up by the Church of England in April 1988 in response to the 'Faith in the City' Report - had raised £4.5 million in its first eight months.

The level of voluntary giving in Britain is put into perspective if you compare these figures with the government Social Fund's current ceiling of over £200 million. Yet as the Social Fund's allocation is reduced, charities will increasingly be expected to make up the shortfall meeting welfare needs and services.

One way of assessing the 'trickle-down theory' is to see whether the poor have actually become better off, but evidence to date offers little to confirm the theory. Between 1978 and 1987 personal disposable income *per capita* in Britain rose by 122% in money terms, or by 14% in real terms. However, during the same period Supplementary Benefit levels fell from 61% of disposable income per capita in 1978 to 53% in 1987. The incomes of the poorest groups have not kept up their share of the total disposable income of the nation.

It is often suggested that people will tend to make their donations to local charities which they know and approve of, meeting only certain perceived local needs. On the other hand, it could be suggested that with the global extension of the concept of community and increased awareness of absolute poverty in third world countries, people's attention is often directed away from the needs of the relatively poor in Britain. It may be that people are more likely to overlook domestic needs in a political climate which stresses individual achievement and explains poverty in terms of individual inadequacy. The distribution of resources in relation to need, then, is a significant issue in itself.

The British public has often responded very generously to various emergency charitable appeals (e.g. the Hillsborough Disaster Fund recently raised £12 million - a record for disaster funds in the UK). But a large-scale shift away from state welfare provision as of right, to *ad hoc* charity would have profound political implications. Charitable activity which increasingly filled in gaps in state provision could be interpreted as a legitimation of an unfair system of distribution, detracting from what has long been agreed as a government responsibility to fulfil the rights of the needy. It is not just a question of the changing balance between state and charitable provision. Of central importance is the fact that there is a qualitative difference between erratic and haphazard charitable relief and statutory services provided in recognition of the belief that, as citizens, individuals have a right to a certain minimum standard of living. It has also been argued that charity creates dependence by relying on the whims of goodwill, reinforcing a patronising approach to disadvantage. On practical as well as ideological grounds critics have suggested that charities will not be able to compensate for the reduction in government expenditure. By itself the voluntary movement cannot provide an adequate substitute for state relief. A return to the situation which existed in Britain before the major social reforms of the post Second World War period is no longer possible. With the advance of secularization religious agencies are not able to take on their former role. Policy shifts will have to be implemented over a long-term time period.

The emphasis in the 'trickle-down theory' on those who achieve legitimises a corresponding stigmatisation of those who fail. This can only have divisive effects within society as the gap between rich and poor widens. From a loss of a sense of community follows a diminishing sense of responsibility to the community. The implications for charity become clear. As the British prime minister, Mrs. Thatcher put it, 'There is no such thing as society; there are individual men and women and there are families' (*Woman's Own*: 31/10/87). That comment prompted many responses, including a number from church leaders. The Anglican and Roman Catholic Bishops of Liverpool have written of the moral implications of deepening divisions. These, they say, threaten our sense of common life: 'When that is lost, individualism becomes a destructive drive, indifferent to those left behind' (1987:305).

Charity, then, is not just about giving money, but about how and why and the way it is given. How can an appeal be made to people's sense of goodness when they will see no direct return from their giving? For the New Right the case for meeting needs through charity follows from the logic of competition within the free market as a means of channelling the efforts of potentially selfish individuals into the service of their fellows. David Green argues that this moral element is central to the legitimation of a liberal approach. He says:

> a free society is only supportable if its adherents advocate a moral code which, among other things, constrains the pursuit of selfish gain and requires the successful to help the less fortunate (1987:218).

He claims that the free market promotes this sense of universal service. Le Grand and Robinson suggest, by contrast, that the principle of the free market promotes selfishness not generosity and that the market fosters attributes such as greed and lack of concern for one's neighbour (1984:267).

This debate about the workability of the 'trickle-down theory' in terms of the values of the free market economy provides a context for examining the changing ways in which appeals are being made and the effects of this on the givers and receivers of charity.

New Ways of Giving to Charity

In the United Kingdom one relatively new method of appeal, apart from telethons, is for charities to buy time for television advertising. The BBC and ITV have for some time given air-time free for charities on 2,000 or so television and radio programmes or items each year. These not only encourage donations, but also give information and advice and recruit volunteers. The cost of a single forty second peak air-time commercial could be as much as £100,000, beyond the reach of all but the biggest charities. After much debate the Independent Broadcasting Authority which controls advertising on the commercial channels has recently (late 1989) permitted charities to buy television advertising. Charities now face the dilemma of whether to try to raise as much money as possible in the short-term or consider the longer-term effects now. In advertising for animal welfare charities, such as the RSPCA, the use of emotive images might be acceptable, but it would be considered by some to be inappropriate, in raising money for famine relief, for example. Images of hopeless, helpless people have tended to foster a patronising response from donors, reinforcing a relationship of dependency rather than explaining and campaigning against the causes of famine and poverty.

Another new mechanism for giving to charities is through 'affinity' credit cards, now being introduced by banks and building societies. For each new applicant accepted, the card company makes an initial donation to the charity of £5 or so and then a further 25p for every £100 spent with the card. The first affinity card to be introduced in Britain was the Bank of Scotland's Visa, which gives to the NSPCC. It has now been joined by many other cards, including TSB Trustcard (linked with Save the Children Fund), Leeds Permanent Building Society (linked with Imperial Cancer Research, Mencap and British Heart Foundation), and Girobank Visa (linked with Oxfam). For cardholders these schemes provide a simple cost-free method of giving to charity. The card companies still make a profit, and charities benefit by receiving regular automatic contributions (at present 83% of giving is spontaneous), in an arrangement which is unlikely to be cancelled. Credit card companies can exploit affinity cards to legitimise their profits, presenting a 'caring' face of capitalism, in contrast to more aggressive marketing tactics. However the further development of affinity cards has recently been threatened by the Customs and Excise Department charging value-added tax on such donations.

Moreover some charities have objected to affinity cards, claiming that banks try to apply pressure for access to charities' mailing lists, and many charities do not like to be associated with schemes encouraging people to go into debt, so reinforcing poverty. Similar schemes have involved companies promoting their products in association with popular charities, working on the idea that sales improve if people feel that some of the profits are going to a good cause. For example, London's Great Ormond Street Hospital 'Wishing Well' Appeal had joint promotions with Mars, Kodak, Hula Hoops, Crown Paints and Volvo.

Christian Ethics and Social Welfare

The changing welfare culture has revived an old debate on the balance between state intervention and voluntarism in welfare provision, and the rights and responsibilities of the well-off in relation to the powerless in society. These ethical questions have always made welfare a contentious issue. The continuing problem of the legitimation of welfare services may be related to the declining relevance of religious values. Such an interpretation would concur with Pinker's conclusion that the tradition of social welfare is a positive expression of 'human altruism, albeit tempered with judicious self-regard. It is part of that desire in human beings to become nobler than they would otherwise be in a state of nature and of their wish to avoid the greater evils of moral anarchy' (1971:212). Christianity has always presented a comprehensive and explicit moral code for social life and certainly a concern for the poor and needy has been a pervasive theme in Christian history. Organised care for the poor, orphans, crippled and sick was not only a practice of the early Church but has continued throughout the centuries. This reflects the fundamental Christian ethic of concern as underlined in the parable of the sheep and goats (Mt.25:31-46), where judgement rested on the criterion of altruistic concern for the suffering. This ethic of active concern as an expression of the love of fellow man is clearly present in the Old Testament also, where the commandment to 'love thy neighbour as thyself' (Lev.19:18) demands corporal works of mercy. As a matter of practice the notion of charity was clearly prevalent in the Hebraic tradition, where one tenth of earnings was linked to the tax system for charitable purposes. The first Christian community held almsgiving in high esteem (Acts 2:44; 4:34-7), while at St. Paul's suggestion the better-off communities collected alms for the poor community of Jerusalem (2 Cor. 8-9). As the unifying link between the realm of religious life and man's commitment in the world, therefore, the emphasis within love is always on action as a condition of loving (1 Jn 4:20). The conception of love, therefore, implies action towards those in situations of need as a special priority, a specific duty.

In terms of legitimising welfare practices, however, the Christian approach to the poor has always been ambiguous. The Christian ethic has been variously defined and applied at different times and in different social and political contexts. Green (1988), for example, outlines how individualism developed as a religious and moral code amongst religious sects during the Reformation. The idea of individual responsibility for personal salvation, self-government and mutual aid contrasted sharply with the Catholic tradition in which the sacraments and hierarchical Church authority were central. Today the approach of many of the churches to social welfare has undergone a transformation, from an emphasis on individual charity and private morality to corporate Church welfare programmes stressing the Christian concepts of community and service.

The tension between individual and collective responsibility for welfare has been a significant feature in the development of social policy in Britain. Thus, for example, the selectivist services of the early twentieth century reflected the moral assumptions of the nineteenth century and the Poor Law, whereby poverty was seen as the responsibility of the individual rather than society. By contrast, the 1944 Beveridge Report introduced a universalist approach, extending the concept of statutory services beyond particular occupational and income groups. Social policy has reflected the realisation that poverty is not a problem of individual character, but of economic and industrial organisation. At stake in questions of social policy are not just the most technically efficient or the cheapest means of reaching an agreed end, but the very nature of the society being sought after. As Pinker puts it, 'We are concerned not only with an economic problem of finding the necessary resources, but with a moral debate as to whether or not they ought to be found' (1978:32).

He maintains that altruism is too rare to serve as a viable basis for social policies, implying that charity could never take over and adequately fulfil the role now provided by the welfare state. Yet statutory welfare services are rooted in altruistic and philanthropic values: 'The generally accepted hallmark of social service is that of direct concern with the personal well-being of the individual' (Hall 1959: 3-4) and its basis is to be found 'in the obligation a person feels to help another in distress' (1957: 7). Some social policy theorists argue that the emphasis today should be less on altruistic moral justifications and more on rational and pragmatic grounds for welfare in the competition for scarce resources (Cowger and Atherton 1977: 13). This viewpoint reinforces Wilson's perception (1985) that public life is being de-moralised. In all those issues important to the maintenance of the social system there is an increasing dependence on technical and legal constraint at the expense of moral constraint. He further argues that the political institutionalisation of moral grounds may have the paradoxical consequence of absolving individuals from the need to cultivate any sense of political responsibility. In his words:

> If the system presents itself as an agency of care then individuals may take leave to 'care less'... the political institutionalisation of what can be represented as the noblest moral concerns may accompany increased moral insensitivity among the people at large (1985: 329).

Such comments as these illustrate the traditional relationship between religious morality and questions of social policy and the continuing concern about the place of moral values in terms of the relative roles of voluntary and statutory provision. In the light of the government's current attempts to dismantle the welfare state and redefine citizenship in terms of individual responsibility and voluntary giving, Christian principles such as care, justice, equality and community have been employed by both sides to legitimise opposing political positions.

Mrs. Thatcher has sought to demonstrate the compatibility of her policies with Christian ethical principles. In a speech to the Assembly of the Church of Scotland in May 1988, she stressed the values of self-reliance and personal responsibility as a Christian moral duty, quoting St. Paul, 'If a man will not work he shall not eat.' This she allied with a moral obligation to others. In her closing speech to the Conservative Party Conference that year, she said 'prosperity has not created the selfish society, but the generous society' and 'personal effort does not undermine the community, it enhances it'.

This philosophy is rooted in a two-fold idea of freedom. On the one hand, freedom refers to the right of the individual to keep the fruits of his labour. This involves a transformation of the Protestant work ethic in which a frugal lifestyle has been replaced by legitimate self-indulgence. Yet at the same time, freedom refers to the right of the individual to give away the fruits of his labour. Government spokesmen argue that if the state takes money away from the individual and so takes on the role of provider, people will not feel any moral sense of obligation:

> Charitable effort is commanded in the Gospels, and has been embodied in the Church's social teaching through the centuries. Individual citizens must remember that their public obligations do not end with the payment of their taxes. But it is something quite different for an elected politician to compel his fellow-citizens to contribute to what the government decides is a worthy cause. Such a compulsion may well be justified but is not an act of charity (Douglas Hurd, *Church Times* 9/9/88).

For the government, dismantling statutory services is part of the process of encouraging a moral sense of responsibility.

Many Christian leaders have criticised this interpretation of the Christian ethic as selective and distorted. The Anglican and Roman Catholic Bishops of Liverpool, for example, have argued that the government does have a responsibility to indicate where the greatest social needs lie and to make provision for those needs by taxes imposed on the community. They challenge the balance of priorities in the enterprise culture, 'for a preoccupation with wealth creation at the expense of wealth distribution' (1988:295). The Christian notion of the church as the body of Christ and the Biblical concept of the family as an extended network can be used to legitimate social concern.

Other Christian critics have challenged the individualism of the enterprise culture with its marriage between individualism and materialism within the capitalist economy. Newbigin, for example, cites the Biblical denunciation of covetousness on which, he says, such a system depends. He outlines what he calls the 'galloping cancer' of consumerism. Similarly, a Papal Encyclical at the end of 1987 criticised 'this blind submission to pure consumerism.' Although the debate about welfare policy is today couched primarily in political terms, such as citizenship and rights, these examples illustrate how Christian ethics remain significant in underpinning and legitimising alternative political perspectives within the enterprise culture.

Just as the institutional Church is often criticised for 'meddling' in politics, so charity and the work of charitable bodies has traditionally been excluded from the political arena. British charity law states that charities should 'avoid seeking to eliminate social, economic, political or other injustice' and that 'to promote changes in the law or maintenance of the existing law is a political purpose and not charitable.' The words 'charity' and 'aid' conjure up an image of unselfish giving. People tend to give to charity without expecting any direct reward. The reasons for giving to charity are, of course, diverse, ranging from compassion to guilt to affection for a particular cause, so suggesting an emotional rather than a reasoned response. Surveys commissioned by the Charities Aid Foundation confirm this. They indicate that only one sixth of people in Britain plan their giving and that 84% of those questioned on their motives towards charity felt that 'it was rewarding to feel you've helped people in need in some way.'

The reality of social need, however, is far from being an apolitical issue. The amount of third world aid channelled through organisations like Oxfam is tiny compared with the overall means of wealth flow from rich to poor countries. This is often used to exercise political influence in third world countries, while the aid itself is frequently insufficiently geared to long-term development. In Britain, charitable agencies responding to the present climate of welfare are starting to highlight the political reasons for poverty and inequality. They are shifting their image from benign philanthropy to that of highly professional campaigning organisations and have joined forces to protest against aspects of government policy which adversely affect their client groups. Hence though nominally apolitical, concern for the needs and rights of the powerless draws caring work into politics. In this sense the Church's work becomes 'political' as it responds to government policy through a needs-based and community-based approach, as illustrated by the *Faith in the City* Report.

Conclusion

In a so-called 'advanced' free market capitalist society such as contemporary Britain, fundamental questions remain about human rights and responsibilities. In terms of giving and receiving, the enterprise culture stresses individualism - individual giving in response to perceived individual need, rather than collective public provision for structural injustice. The current government legitimises its policies by reference to Christian morality and the 'trickle-down theory', but whether the 'trickle-down theory' is workable in practice has not yet been adequately shown. So far what has been seen is a reduction in direct government commitment to the needy, matched by increasingly heavy demands on the voluntary sector. It is ironic that at a time when the churches have fewer members and fewer resources, people are once more turning to parishes and charities for help, reinforcing a sense of stigma and dependence on goodwill for fulfilling fundamental needs.

Bibliography

BBC Television 1988, transcripts 'Heart of the Matter', (13 & 20 March).

Cowger, D and Atherton, C 1977 'Social Control: A Rationale for Social Welfare', in Fitzgerald, M (ed) 1977 *Welfare in Action*, London: Routledge and Kegan Paul.

Church of England General Synod, 1985 *Faith in the City: a Call for Action by Church and Nation*, London: Church House Publishing.

Green, D 1988 *The New Right*, Brighton: Wheatsheaf Books.

Hall, P 1959 *The Social Services of Modern England*, London: Routledge and Kegan Paul.

Le Grand, J and Robinson, R 1983 *The Economics of Social Problems*, London: Macmillan.

Newbigin, L 1985 'The Welfare State: A Christian Perspective', *Theology*, 88: 173-81.

Pinker, R 1971 *Social Theory and Social Policy*, London: Heinemann.

Pinker, R 1978 *Research Priorities in the Personal Social Services*, London: Social Science Research Council.

Sheppard, D and Worlock, D 1989 *Better Together*, London: Penguin.

Titmuss, R 1958 *Essays on the Welfare State*, London: Allen and Unwin.

Townsend, P 1968 *Social Services for All - Part One*, London: Fabian Society Tract No.382.

Wilson, B R 1985 'Morality in the Evolution of the Social System', *British Journal of Sociology*, 36: 315-32.

Wogaman, J P 1976 *A Christian Method of Moral Judgement*, London: SCM Press.

5
Enjoying God Forever:
An Historical/Sociological Profile
of the Health and Wealth Gospel
in the U.S.A

Dennis Hollinger

The 1647 Westminster Catechism begins with the question, 'What is the chief end of man?' The catechist responds, 'Man's chief end is to glorify God and to enjoy Him forever' (General Assembly 1966, section 7.001). Throughout the church's history, certain groups and movements have tended to over-emphasize one dimension of this response at the expense of the other. The health and wealth gospel appears to be a case in point. By accentuating the goodness of God (which is activated by a believer's faith) the movement's adherents are inclined to focus primarily on enjoying God over glorifying God. Evidence for the theme of enjoyment is seen in the promises of healing, financial prosperity and general well-being.

The health and wealth gospel in the United States is an identifiable religious movement comprised of distinct teachings, key preachers, a particular clientele, conferences, massive publications, media ministries, local congregations that identify with the teachings and preachers, educational institutions and a loosely-knit organization called the International Convention of Faith Churches and Ministries (ICFCM). Adherents have often labelled themselves 'Word' or 'Word of Faith' Churches as well as 'faith movement.' Critics have utilized such phrases as 'name it and claim it', 'the gospel of prosperity', and 'the health and wealth gospel.' Among the major leaders are Kenneth Hagin, Kenneth and Gloria Copeland, Jerry Savelle, and Fred Price - people with substantial followings not only in the United States but also in parts of Europe and the Third World. All reflect strong charismatic leadership qualities and all have gone through rather traumatic physical, and/or financial crises at some point in their lives. The themes of the movement are certainly not new. The emphasis, for example, on financial prosperity being a fruit of true Christian commitment, prayer or faith has precedence within Christian history. During the Gilded Age in late nineteenth-century America numerous clergy espoused the notion that right thinking and right living could unlock the doors to bountiful wealth. William Lawrence (1858-1941), an Episcopalian Bishop of Massachusetts, taught that 'in the long run, it is only to the man of morality that wealth comes... Godliness is in league with riches' (Lawrence 1966:331). Russell Conwell (1843-1925), a Baptist clergyman and founder of Temple University, delivered his famous 'Acres of Diamonds' lecture over six thousand times to audiences hungry to hear the message that wealth could be found in positive thinking and righteous living.   Similar notions have appeared in cross-cultural expressions of 'Christianity' such as Cargo Cults.   What is new among the contemporary faith teachers is the particular way in which they have packaged and framed their beliefs.   Their roots and ideas can certainly be found in prior movements and historic figures, but the health and wealth gospel clearly represents a new and distinct religious movement which is flourishing amidst the controversy which surrounds it.

This essay seeks to give an historical and sociological overview of the faith movement.   After a brief overview of its major themes, we will probe its historic roots, and then finally provide some possible sociological reasons as to why the health and wealth gospel has emerged and flourished in twentieth-century America.

Major Themes

According to Bruce Barron (1987:9), there are three main themes which set the movement apart from traditional Christian understandings: healing, prosperity and positive confession. The faith teachers themselves are quick to point out that these are not the primary themes of Christian faith and that they must be understood in light of traditional Christian doctrines. Kenneth Hagin Jr., in a personal letter, rejected any cultic or heresy labels and stated, 'Our major tenets of faith are held in common by those in the evangelical world - beliefs such as the virgin birth and deity of our Lord Jesus Christ, the absolute necessity of the new birth through faith in the atoning work of Jesus on the cross, and other fundamental doctrines of the church.' Nonetheless, the themes of healing, prosperity and public confession are highly significant for faith preachers and their followers and are clearly at the heart of the controversy surrounding the movement.

The themes themselves are generally understood to have their source in the Abrahamic covenant with its promise of great blessing.   In the Old Testament these blessings included health and wealth to those who were faithful to God.   The atonement of Christ is seen to extend these blessings to all people on the basis of Galatians 3:13-14, 'Christ redeemed us from the curse of the law... that the blessing of Abraham might come to the Gentiles through Christ' (New International Version).   As Kenneth Copeland puts it, 'You are an heir to the blessing which God gave to Abraham.   This blessing, found in the 28th chapter of Deuteronomy, covers every area of your existence: spirit, soul, body, financially, and socially' (Copeland 1979a:22).   Not only does Christ's atonement extend Abraham's blessings to us, it also overturns the curse of the law, which included both poverty and sickness.   It is from this framework that the faith teachers espouse healing, prosperity and positive confession.

Healing

Divine healing is by no means a novel teaching. Christian theologians, preachers, and movements down through history have articulated in varying forms doctrines of healing. What sets the health and wealth gospel apart from mainstream Christian understanding is its emphatic insistence that God always intends to heal, and that healing is assured if Christians have the faith to believe it. Most of the movement's teachers do not totally negate the role of the medical profession, but insist that divine healing is a higher way. As Fred Price put it, 'Doctors are fighting the same enemies that we are, the only difference is they're using toothpicks and we are using atomic bombs' (Price 1976:113). One exception to a secondary acceptance of medical help was the late Hobart Freeman, who while not being closely connected organizationally to the other faith preachers, nevertheless shared with them similar teachings. Freeman forbade any medical help for his followers, including eye glasses, and came to the national spotlight when it was reported that by 1984 over ninety unnecessary deaths had occurred in his Faith Assembly movement (Barron 1987).

The faith teachers believe that 'healing is just as much a part of the plan of redemption as salvation, the Holy Spirit and heaven as your eternal home' (Copeland 1979b:7). Since healing is perceived to be accomplished through Christ's atonement, it is activated by faith alone. While the laying on of hands has been utilized in their healing campaigns, these preachers are quick to note that there is no power of healing in this symbolic act. Rather the ritual is a point of contact with someone who has faith in order to activate the faith of the person in need. The health and wealth gospel's doctrine of healing is clearly stated by Jerry Savelle:

> Not only is it God's will to heal, it is God's will to heal all! Satan is the author of sickness and disease. By the authority of His Word, God has made provision for our healing. It is not the will of God that anyone be sick with any sickness or disease or pain whatsoever - from hang-nails to tuberculosis! (Savelle 1981:8).

Prosperity

The doctrine of prosperity, while being the most controversial of the movement's teachings, has certainly been a major factor in its popularity. The concept is understood in broad terms: 'Prosperity is the condition of being successful and thriving in all areas: spiritually strong, physically strong (healthy), and mentally solid' (Willis n.d:15). But there is no question that for the faith adherents financial prosperity is a divine promise signifying God's blessing upon those whose faith is great enough to expect it.

Since material wealth was part of the Abrahamic covenant and since Christ has overturned the curse of the law which included poverty, Christians are said to have a right to claim prosperity. Moreover, says Fred Price, 'If the Mafia can ride around in Lincoln Continental town cars, why

can't Kings's Kids?' (Price 1979:34). The adherents find further support in
the New Testament with passages like the King James Version rendition of
3 John 2, 'Beloved, I wish above all things that thou mayest prosper and
be in health, even as thy soul prospereth.'

Some of the faith preachers advocate a 'success formula' which they
assert to be a universal or cosmic law. Essentially the formula claims that
financial success will come to those who have the faith to believe it and
who are themselves a giving people. Since it is a universal law it is
bestowed even to non-Christians who practice its principles. Speaking of
a non-believer who did so Kenneth Hagin writes, 'God didn't bless him
because he was a sinner. He received God's blessing because he honored
God. God has a certain law of prosperity and when you get into contact
with that law... it just works for you - whoever you are' (Hagin 1974:2).

Part of the 'success formula' is the promise of an hundredfold return
based on Mark 10:29-30: 'No one who has left home or brothers or sisters
or mother or father or children or fields for me and the gospel will fail to
receive a hundred times as much in this present age (homes, brothers,
sisters, mothers, children and fields - and with them, persecutions) and in
the age to come, eternal life' (NIV).

Commenting on this passage Gordon Lindsay of Christ for the Nations
Institute in Dallas says, 'There can be no mistake, the promise includes
temporal wealth.... How much? An hundred fold! In other words he who
gives up thousands in following Christ is eligible to receive hundreds of
thousands' (Lindsay 1959:46). In similar fashion Kenneth Copeland asks,
'Do you want a hundredfold return on your money? Give and let God
multiply it back to you' (Copeland 1974:67).

Many of the faith teachers clearly articulate that the divine promise of
financial reward is not for personal selfishness or greed, but rather is
granted by God for the purposes of generosity towards others and the
propagation of the faith. As Gloria Copeland puts it: 'Don't just believe
God to meet your needs. Believe Him for a surplus of prosperity so that
you can help others. We here in America are a blessed people financially.
We have been called to finance the gospel to the world' (Copeland 1978:45).
Kenneth Hagin Jr. has responded with disgust towards those who follow
the movement in order to get wealthy. Speaking to a gathering of students
at his Rhema Bible Training Center he asserted boldly, 'If you came to this
school with the idea that it is going to help you get more faith so you can
have Cadillacs, I want you to resign today' (Hagin Jr. 1980:7).

In recent years further qualifications have been placed on the prosperity
theme. For example, since 1985 Kenneth Copeland has acknowledged that
prosperity is relative and in many contexts throughout the world may come
in the forms of bountiful rain and plenty of food (Barron 1987:97). Others
have admitted that their teachings have been taken by followers to
overshadow the main tenets of the Christian faith. Despite such
confessions the movement continues to articulate the theme of prosperity
in a 'kingdom context', for prosperity they believe is clearly promised in the

pages of scripture. As Jerry Savelle puts it, 'If I am not prospering... it is not God's fault, nor the fault of the Word of God - it is my fault' (Savelle 1982:77).

Positive Confession

According to the faith movement, healing and prosperity are primarily realized through the third distinctive theme, positive confession. This concept can best be understood as a statement, made in faith, that lays claim to God's provisions and promises. To be healed, for example, a person must pray in faith with a positive affirmation that they are healed, even if the symptoms of illness linger on. Since it is 'with your mouth that you confess and are saved' (Romans 10:10), it is with similar confession that humans can experience and enjoy God's other provisions. Positive confession is also seen to be grounded in Mark 11:23-24: 'I tell you the truth, if anyone says to this mountain, "Go, throw yourself into the sea," and does not doubt in his heart but believes that what he says will happen, it will be done for him. Therefore I tell you, whatever you ask for in prayer, believe that you have received it, and it will be yours' (NIV).

It is from this theme that the popular phrase, 'Name it and claim it' is derived. In a widely circulated booklet Kenneth Hagin unabashedly affirms, 'You can have what you say.' Hagin goes on to note that people's 'words give them away. You can locate people by what they say. Their confession locates them' (Hagin 1979:6). Though Hagin puts some limits on what we can request from God, he also speaks forthrightly of writing your own ticket with God. He asserts that God has given to him four simple steps - say it, do it, receive it and tell it - which will enable anyone to receive from God what they confess (Hagin 1983:76). Kenneth Copeland describes this theme in terms of commanding God:

> As a believer, you have a right to make commands in the name of Jesus. Each time you stand on the Word, you are commanding God to a certain extent because it is His Word. Whenever an honest man gives you his word, he is bound by it. It is not necessary to order him around because a truly honest man will back his word. When you stand on what he has said, he is commanded to do it (Copeland 1976:32).

Positive confession then is the vehicle through which God's promises are effected for the faith preachers. To pray 'If it be God's will,' reflects a lack of faith and positive confession. Charles Capps, a retired farmer and now a leading exponent of the movement, states, 'You have to believe that those things you say - everything you say - will come to pass. That will activate the God kind of faith within you, and those things which you say will come to pass' (Capps 1976:24).

Historical Roots: Pentecostal Healing Revivalism

The contemporary health and wealth gospel movement flows historically from two primary tributaries: Pentecostal healing revivalism and the influence of E.W. Kenyon (1867-1948), a New England preacher-educator who apparently imbibed at the waters of nineteenth-century New Thought metaphysics. D.R. McConnell's recent work, *A Different Gospel*, attempts to undermine the Pentecostal influence and focus only on the 'Kenyon Connection'. My own conclusion, however, is that we cannot minimize the role of the healing revivalist tradition.

Pentecostalism in America is generally recognized as having emerged with the Azusa Street Revival in Los Angeles, 1906. Expanding on the earlier holiness emphases on a second work of grace and entire sanctification, Pentecostalism stressed the need for a baptism of the Holy Spirit evidenced by speaking in tongues. Healing and other miraculous signs were at the heart of the movement from its earliest days. Numerous faith healers travelled the pentecostalist circuit with a message that faith and the touch of the healer could evoke a miracle from God.

It was not, however, until after World War II that a distinct healing revival movement emerged. David Harrell describes it this way:

> Since World War II, hundreds of ministers, most of them in the 1950s coming from the ranks of classical pentecostalism but later from a variety of backgrounds, established independent evangelistic associations. These associations lived or died with the charisma of the evangelist, and some became multimillion dollar organizations. Taken together, they were a powerful independent force in modern American religion and won the religious loyalty and financial support of millions of Americans. Little understood by the public, the faith healing revivalists were the main actors in the postwar pentecostal drama (Harrell 1975:4).

Among the key figures of this movement were William Branham, Oral Roberts, Jack Coe, A.A. Allen, Gordon Lindsay, and T.L. Osborn. The ministry of these and similar healing revivalists received coverage in *The Voice of Healing*, a magazine which more than any other vehicle tied the entire movement together. The revivalists were essentially of one mind with regards to healing - God always intends to heal and it is up to the faith of the believer, activated by the laying on of hands or by anointed-cloths, to bring God's promise to fruition.

The theme of prosperity is found early on in the healing revival movement. Already in the 1930s a Thomas Wyatt made prosperity the foundation of his ministry (Harrell 1975:229). In the 1950s the controversial A.A. Allen began to accentuate the financial blessing theme. Allen, who eventually died from alcoholism, was fond of telling a story about a $410 printing bill which he couldn't pay. He had only a few one-dollar bills in his pocket when suddenly the bills were transformed to twenties and the need was met. In 1963 Allen claimed to have received a revelation directly from God: 'I am a wealthy God! Yea, I am not poor... But I say unto thee, claim my wealth in thy hand, yea, in thy purse and in thy substance. For behold, I plan to do a new thing in the earth!' (Allen 1963:i-ii).

In 1947 Oral Roberts 'discovered' 3 John:2 with its perceived emphasis on prosperity. Commenting on the passage he said to his wife, 'Evelyn, we have been wrong. I haven't been preaching that God is good. And Evelyn, if this verse is right, God is a good God.' David Harrell notes that from this point the Roberts began to explore the implications of such a message not only for a new car, house etc. but also for their larger world-wide ministry (Harrell 1985:66).

The prosperity theme of the revivalists was often placed in the service of fund-raising, and therein emerged considerable controversy. Already in the early 1950s the Assemblies of God leadership began to raise questions about such fund-raising efforts and their corresponding themes of prosperity. By 1953 the denomination's *Pentecostal Evangel* stopped printing the revivalists' reports, and three years later their General Presbytery issued a strongly-worded statement against questionable fund-raising techniques and promises of financial reward (Harrell 1975:108-9). Clearly then, the emphasis on prosperity among contemporary faith teachers is nothing new.

By the late 1950s as the healing revival movement began to wane, a new movement was about to be born - the new Charismatic movement. This burgeoning religious force came to replace the old-style Pentecostalism in popularity and influence. Some of the old-time healing revivalists made the transition to a less separatistic and less legalistic expression of faith; others did not. Among those who made the transition was Kenneth Hagin, now generally regarded as the major figure of the faith movement. As Bruce Barron sees it, the faith teachers 'owe their success largely to their transformation from Pentecostal to charismatic' (1987:11). The contemporary health and wealth gospel emphasis is linked to the older pentecostal healing revivalism both through ideas (i.e. healing, faith, prosperity) as well as through individuals who bridged the two movements, such as Kenneth Hagin.

Another significant figure to make that transition was Oral Roberts. Of interest at this point is his role in the faith movement. There are clear links between Roberts and the faith teachers, but striking differences as well. We have already noted that in 1947 Roberts got excited over the 3 John:2 passage with its perceived implications for prosperity. In 1954 he introduced the 'Blessing-Pact', with a promised financial blessing for those who gave $100 to his ministry. A year later he published *God's Formula for Success and Prosperity* and in the 1970s he began teaching his 'seed-faith' concept. With this latter idea Roberts taught that the Old Testament tithe (give because you owe it to God) was replaced in the New Testament with giving in order to expect a blessing. God will supply, said

Roberts, not just the bare essentials of life, but will give abundantly to those who give.

Not only have some of Roberts' ideas seemed similar to the faith teachers, but he has also had intimate contact with them. Roberts has often attended and preached at Kenneth Hagin's annual camp-meeting and has invited numerous of the faith teachers to preach at Oral Roberts University. Controversy over their message peaked in 1980 when Fred Price was preaching at ORU and a theology professor shouted 'No' in response to Price's teaching. Roberts was incensed by the protest and demanded an apology from the professor (Harrell 1985:423-7).

Despite the personal interactions and similar ideas Oral Roberts seems to have distanced himself from the movement at certain points and is continuing to distance himself as the controversy intensifies. Roberts, for example, does not teach that God will always heal if one only believes and positively confesses. His own City of Faith (now defunct) blended medical healing with faith. In an article on faith healing in *Christianity Today* Rodney Clapp notes, 'In visiting places like... Oral Robert's City of Faith hospital, I detected the unfolding of what I call a centrist view of healing' (Clapp 1983:13). It is also significant to note that some of the sharpest critiques of the faith movement have come from within the university, namely ORU Theology Professor Charles Farah's *From the Pinnacle of the Temple* and McConnell's *A Different Gospel*, originally a Master's thesis at ORU. Roberts, like other faith teachers bridged the gap between the older pentecostal healing movement and the newer charismatic expression. At best, however, his link to the health and wealth gospel remains tentative.

Historical Roots: The Role of E.W. Kenyon

It might appear unlikely that a New England preacher-educator with no organizational or personal links to Pentecostalism could influence a movement such as the health and wealth gospel. But there is undeniable evidence that E.W. Kenyon has played a formative role in the ideas propagated by faith preachers. D. R. McConnell's book demonstrates how Kenyon's ideas have directly shaped the thought of faith teachers, and how Kenyon himself had been strongly influenced by New Thought metaphysics or Science of the Mind, a philosophy quite prevalent in late nineteenth-century New England as Kenyon was beginning his ministry. Writing primarily to refute theologically faith teachings, McConnell can be vitriolic at times and is reluctant to acknowledge Pentecostal healing revivalism as one of the roots of the faith movement, but his work is extremely valuable in documenting the 'Kenyon connection.'

Born on April 24, 1867 in Saratoga County New York, Essek William Kenyon became a self-educated student and avid supporter of education. He never earned a degree, but attended various institutions in New Hampshire and Boston. Though he was raised a Methodist, Kenyon joined the Baptists following his conversion during late adolescence. He became an evangelist and through his preaching helped start a number of Baptist churches in rural New England. Kenyon's zeal for education led him to found Bethel Bible Institute in Spencer, Massachusetts, a school that eventually became Barrington College (now merged with Gordon College). He was the superintendent and driving force behind Bethel from 1900 to 1923, but eventually resigned from the school amidst a swirl of controversy which was never made public. From there Kenyon moved to the West Coast where he pastored several churches, served as an itinerant evangelist, carried on a radio program, and wrote books and pamphlets until his death in 1948.

While living in Boston in the 1890s Kenyon attended the Emerson College of Oratory, a school that was closely connected with New Thought metaphysics. 'New Thought was the brainchild of Phineas P. Quimby (1802-66)... and it is generally agreed by scholars of the metaphysical cults that Mary Baker Eddy, the founder of Christian Science, was heavily dependent on the writings of P.P. Quimby, by whom she received a healing and under whom she later studied' (McConnell 1988:34).

A broad movement involving numerous metaphysical groups, New Thought accentuated among other things the immanence of God, the primacy of the mind as a cause of all effects, freedom from disease and poverty, the divine nature of humans, and the role of incorrect thinking in all sin and disease. McConnell believes that though Kenyon at times criticised the New Thought movement he nonetheless drank deeply at its wells through his studies at Emerson College as well as through contacts with various people in Boston who had propensities in that direction. He writes, 'Because he had no theological background in... the Holiness-Pentecostal tradition, in formulating his 'new type of Christianity' of healing and prosperity, Kenyon drew from the only background in these areas that he did have: metaphysics' (McConnell 1988:49).

Kenyon's preaching reverberated with themes we have noted in the health and wealth gospel: healing, prosperity and positive confession. Of the latter, for example, Kenyon taught that what one confesses with the lips controls one's inner being. In fact Kenyon is the source of the popular phrase in the faith movement, 'What I confess, I possess' (Kenyon 1970:88). Teaching that sickness is spiritual not physical, Kenyon stated, 'I know that I am healed because He said that I am healed and it makes no difference what the symptoms may be in the body. I laugh at them, and in the Name of Jesus I command the author of the disease to leave my body' (Kenyon 1970:99). He also emphasized prosperity but was less materialistic in his understanding of it than the current faith movement. Kenyon was not a Pentecostalist and even saw destructive tendencies in pentecostal teaching. Nonetheless, various of the Pentecostal healing revivalists of the 1940s and 50s had read Kenyon's works extensively and at times quoted from him. As the metamorphosis evolved from old-time healing revivalism to the new faith movement, one person more than any other propagated certain of Kenyon's emphases - Kenneth Hagin. Hagin has on occasion acknowledged his appreciation of Kenyon's writings, but McConnell shows far more extensive borrowing from Kenyon than Hagin admits. In fact McConnell documents extensive plagiarism by Hagin from Kenyon. His book contains four pages of column by column comparison of Kenyon and Hagin quotes and the evidence is overwhelming - it is virtually word for word borrowing without any acknowledgment. Hagin's plagiarism is contained in numerous articles and books over a period of eight years (McConnell 1988:8-12).

The use of Kenyon by the faith teachers has not gone unnoticed by those who were once close to the evangelist-educator. Speaking of the faith movement's little acknowledged use of her fathers ideas, Kenyon's own daughter, Ruth Kenyon Houseworth, said, 'His first book was printed in 1916, and he had the revelation years before that. These that are coming along now that have been in the ministry for just a few years and claiming that this is something that they are just starting, it makes you laugh a little bit' (McConnell 1988:5). Similarly, John Kennington, a pastor in Oregon who knew and on occasion ministered with Kenyon, states, 'Today Kenyon's ideas are in the ascendancy. Via the electronic church or in the printed page I readily recognize not only Kenyon's concepts, but at times I recognize pure plagiarism, for I can almost tell you book, chapter, and page where the material is coming from' (*ibid.*). The role of E.W. Kenyon in the health and wealth gospel is undeniable. Though Kenyon's link with the New Thought movement needs further historical investigation, McConnell's attempt to show the connection seems quite persuasive.

A Sociological Analysis

In this brief sociological analysis I intend only to suggest some possible human explanations for the contemporary popularity, forms and emphases of the health and wealth gospel. The following are only representative of the kinds of sociological explanations that might be offered to explain the movement's development. Others could undoubtedly be added to the list.

One possible explanation for the popularity and particular emphases of the faith movement is **relative deprivation theory**. It hypothesizes that 'people join sects because they seek to redress the lack of deference and esteem they feel is rightfully theirs' (Schwartz 1970:40-41). The deprivation or marginality perceived by such people may be economic, cultural, or psychological, but joining a particular religious group is one way to establish one's niche within society. By itself the theory is an insufficient explanation for human behaviour, for it does not account for a number of realities: why people join one movement over another, why some people look to religion and others do not, and why the most disadvantaged in society often refuse to join organized religious groups at all. But deprivation can be seen as one salient factor among others for explaining religious behaviour and expression. No data is available at this time on the socio-economic status of faith teaching followers, but the assumption of most observers is that they come from the ranks of working-class people who are seeking to find a psychological, economic and cultural home in middle-America. If that is indeed the case we can understand why such persons would be attracted to a movement which holds, in the words of Kenneth Hagin, that God 'wants His children to eat the best, He wants them to wear the best clothing, He wants them to drive the best cars, and He wants them to have the best of everything' (Hagin 1980:54-5).

It is also significant that almost all of the movement's leading preachers either grew up in poverty and hardship or at least at some point in their lives experienced destitution and feelings of powerlessness. R.O. Corvin, an influential Pentecostal leader and educator since World War II, gives some feel of the background from which many of the leaders emerged:

> Persecution against Pentecostals was both real and imaginary. Preachers who identified themselves with the churches entered the arena of life fighting... They preached in school houses, under brush arbors, in store buildings, on street corners, under tents, in homes, on radios. They built inferior frame structures and large tabernacles (Corvin 1971:12).

Coming from such marginal contexts, the faith preachers have often despised their early poverty and deprivation. A gospel of economic and physical well-being was appealing to such persons and continues to provide hope for the thousands of followers who seek release from a life of socio-cultural disenfranchisement.

American Cultural Themes

Another possible explanation for the rise of this movement is that it stems from cultural themes that are deeply embedded in American society. Notions of wealth and health (physical well-being) have long and powerful histories in this society, and it is therefore understandable that at times these values have become integral parts of religious expression. Like deprivation, these contextual themes alone cannot account for a movement, but they might coalesce with other explanatory variables.

Americans have historically been concerned with physical well-being, a passion that likely contributed in part to the rise of New Thought metaphysics (including Christian Science) in the nineteenth century. Two recent books describe the current American preoccupation with wellness and our bodies: *Worried Sick: Our Troubled Quest for Wellness* by Arthur J. Barsky, and *Bodies: Why We Look the Way We Do (And How We Feel About It)* by sociologist Barry Glassner. Barsky, a professor of psychiatry at Harvard Medical School, observes that 'because health has become synonymous with overall well-being, it has become an end in itself, a paramount aim of life' (*Time* 1988:66). Could it be that the health and wealth gospel is a reflection of such an ethos? Similarly, wealth and prosperity have been part of the American character for centuries. Some of the earliest European descriptions of the New World focused primarily on its wealth and economic opportunity. In *Eastward Ho*, a comedy written in 1605, one of the characters says of Virginia, 'I tell thee, gold is more plentiful there than copper is with us.... Why, man, all their dripping pans are pure gold; and all their chains with which they chain up their streets are massy gold'. As David Potter writes:

> The factor of abundance, which we first discovered as an environmental condition and which we then converted by technological change into a cultural as well as a physical force, has not only influenced all the aspects of American life in a fundamental way but has also impinged upon our relations with the peoples of the world (1954:141).

Countless other analysts have described the profound impact that the pursuit of wealth and prosperity have had on American social character. It would appear that the contemporary faith movement is another chapter in that cultural history.

The thrust of the health and wealth gospel is also a reflection of another American cultural theme, individualism. In Robert Bellah's widely read *Habits of the Heart*, personal fulfilment and financial success are portrayed as major expressions of the American ethos of individualism: 'Americans tend to think of the ultimate goals of a good life as matters of personal choice. The means to achieve individual choice, they tend to think, depend on economic progress' (Bellah 1985:22). Such attitudes have become commonplace in American religion with its privatized, therapeutic bent which often seeks not the good of others, but primarily the good of the self. Its narcissistic tendencies are well captured by Bellah in an interview with a young nurse named Sheila: 'My faith has carried me a long way. It's Sheilaism. Just my own little voice... It's just try to love yourself and be gentle with yourself' (Bellah 1985:221). While the faith movement tends to stand over against American culture at one level, at another level it may well have acquiesced to the lure of American individualism and personal success. For it is the enjoyment of God, not the glory of God, which seems to have captivated the hearts and minds of the faith teaching followers.

The Fund Raising Factor

There is a rather pragmatic factor that has likely played a significant role in the prosperity emphasis of the faith teachers, namely their need to raise money to maintain their ministries. As Bruce Barron has noted,

> Many well-known faith teachers do not pastor a church of their own, so they have no list of members whose donations they can count on receiving consistently. If they do not continue to successfully solicit contributions and sell their books and tapes, they have no guaranteed income against which to borrow (Barron 1987:139).

The competition is fierce and the cost of TV programs, satellite networks, and extensive travel is immense. In such a context the temptation to accentuate economic promises for giving to God (via their particular ministry) is overwhelming. From a functionalist perspective, the selected theological distinctiveness of the movement serves to ensure its financial solvency.

As noted earlier, fund-raising tactics that included financial promise received attention and critique already in the 1950s by the leadership of the Assemblies of God. Though some of the faith preachers have attempted to moderate their appeals, others have not. One young health and wealth gospel preacher told his audience:

> Now there are fifteen people here tonight in this tent... because God has told me that he is going to give you an unlimited blessing. God told me that. God is going to speak to fifteen people to write a check, even if you have to postdate it for thirty days. God is going to talk to fifteen people to write a check or give $300.... Now, if you don't believe he can do it for you, then you're not going to be one of them (Harrell 1975:229).

Most faith preachers are not quite so overt, but the covert message can be read between the lines. One can only speculate what would happen to the movement if promises of prosperity and health were suddenly removed.

Conclusion

Enjoying God forever! Proclaimers of the health and wealth gospel appear to be doing just that, at least for the moment. This dynamic and flourishing movement has undoubtedly played a more significant role in shaping the American religious landscape than has been previously acknowledged. Key teachings and tenets have subtly infiltrated the thought and vocabulary of preachers and lay persons not otherwise identified with the movement. Statements like 'You can't outgive God,' and 'God doesn't want his people to go second class', reverberate well beyond the formal boundaries of the movement itself.

The future of the health and wealth gospel is hard to predict. There are signs that certain leaders are beginning to moderate some of their teachings in response to widespread criticism. Simultaneously new preachers and teachers with even more crass approaches are appearing on the scene. What can be said from a sociological standpoint is that the health and wealth gospel resonates in profound ways with some of the deeply embedded cultural themes of American society. Therein lies much of its success.

Bibliography

Allen, A A   1963 *Power To Get Wealth*, Miracle Valley, Arizona: A A Allen Revivals.

Barron, B   1987 *The Health and Wealth Gospel*, Downers Grove, Ill.: InterVarsity Press.

Bellah, R   et al. 1985 *Habits of the Heart: Individualism and Commitment in American Life*, New York: Harper and Row.

Capps, C 1976 *The Tongue: A Creative Force*, Tulsa: Harrison House.

Clapp, R 1983 'Faith Healing: A Look at What's Happening', *Christianity Today* (Dec 16):13.

Copeland, G 1978 *God's Will Is Prosperity*, Tulsa: Harrison House.

Copeland, K 1974 *The Laws of Prosperity*, Ft. Worth: Kenneth Copeland Publications.

Copeland, K 1976 *Our Covenant With God*, Ft. Worth: KCP.

Copeland, K 1979a *Welcome to The Family*, Ft. Worth: KCP.

Copeland, K 1979b *You Are Healed*, Ft. Worth: KCP.

Corvin, R O 1971 'Pentecost in Three Dimensions', *World Pentecost*, 1:12.

General Assembly 1966 *The Book of Confessions*, Philadelphia: General Assembly of the United Presbyterian Church in the USA.

Forell G W 1966 *Christian Social Teachings*, Garden City, N.Y.: Doubleday.

Hagin, K 1974 'The Law of Faith', *Word of Faith*, (Nov): 2.

Hagin, K 1979 *You Can Have What You Say!* Tulsa: Kenneth Hagin Ministries.

Hagin, K 1980 *New Thresholds of Faith*, Tulsa: Faith Library.

Hagin, K 1983 *Exceedingly Growing Faith*, Tulsa: KHM.

Hagin Jr., K 1980 'Victory Words for Front-Line Battles', *The Word of Faith* (Nov): 7.

Harrell, D 1975 *All Things Are Possible: The Healing and Charismatic Revivals in Modern America*, Bloomington: Indiana University Press

Harrell, D 1985 *Oral Roberts: An American Life*, Bloomington: Indiana University Press.

Kenyon, E W 1970 *The Hidden Man: An Unveiling of the Subconscious Mind*, Seattle: Kenyon's Gospel Publ. Society.

Lindsay, G 1959 *God's Master Key to Success and Prosperity*, Dallas: Voice of Healing Publications.

McConnell, D L 1988 *A Different Gospel: A Historical and Biblical Analysis of the Modern Faith Movement*, Peabody, Mass.: Hendrickson.

Potter, D M 1954 *People of Plenty: Economic Abundance and the American Character*, Chicago: University of Chicago Press.

Price, F 1976 *Is Healing for All?* Tulsa: Harrison House.

Price, F 1979 *Faith, Foolishness or Presumption?* Tulsa: Harrison House.

Savelle, J 1981 *God's Provision for Healing*, Tulsa: Harrison House.

Savelle, J 1982 *Living in Divine Prosperity*, Tulsa: Harrison House.

Schwartz, G 1970 *Sect Ideologies and Social Status*, Chicago: University of Chicago Press.

Time 1988 'A Nation of Healthy Worrywarts?' *Time*, (July 25): 66.

Willis, E n.d. *God's Plan For Financial Prosperity*, Lafayette, La: Fill The Gap Publications.

6
The Worldview Orientations of Polish Youth

Halina Grzymala-Moszczynska

Over the past ten years, the findings of research on Polish religiosity have revealed a constant pattern. They have shown a steady increase in religiosity, as indicated by measures of identity and religious practice and by the numbers of self-defined church members. The research has also revealed strong tendencies towards certain types of religiosity, such as selectivity in the area of dogmatic beliefs, a tendency which has been revealed in research in other parts of the world.

Another trend has been the decrease in commitment to atheism, from 17% of the adult population in 1977 to only 5% by 1988. Findings now show that religion in Poland belongs in an equally strong way to two domains, the general national culture and people's private lives. The former remains strongly immune to the processs of secularization and is well supported by feelings of national identity and independence. The latter is changing under the influence of industrialization and urbanization (see Piwowarski 1977, Strassberg 1988).

However, in spite of the abundance of research based on a scientific, hard-data approach, there is hardly any information on the presence in Polish society of aspects of worldviews which go beyond Christian and

Table 1. Proportion of Respondents in Each Educational Category

Type of Establishment	Number	%
Polytechnics	30	12.9
Academies of Art	33	11.9
Universities	39	14.0
Secondary Schools and Colleges	26	9.4
Technical Colleges	30	10.8
Seminaries	41	4.7
Fine Arts Colleges	26	9.4
Oratoria	36	12.9
Missing	11	4.0
TOTAL	278	100.0

atheistic perspectives. Research reports traditionally specify only two choices: the religious, which is mainly Christian, and the non-religious or more clearly defined atheistic alternative. The aim of the present study is to demonstrate the existence within Polish culture of differing and alternative worldviews, to examine a number of the variables related to their adoption and to measure in some degree the relative popularity of these orientations within different sectors of the youth population.

A total sample of 278 respondents from universities, other higher and futher education institutions and secondary schools in two cities, Cracow and Kielce, served as subjects. The sample was neither random nor stratified, though an attempt was made to ensure an adequate representation of students and young adults from various types of educational institution. The research can thus form the basis for further, more sophisticated sample designs in this most under-researched area of worldview orientations. 41% of the subjects were female. The age range for students at university, polytechnic and academies of art was 18-29. For secondary school and further education college students, the age range was 16-22 and for seminarians training for the priesthood 17-20. The group described as attending an Oratorium are those young people between the ages of 17 and 21 who, under supervision of the Roman Catholic Church, work with socially underprivileged young people and with those who have special needs, including drug addicts and the children of alcoholics as well

Table 2. Respondents by Educational Category and Father's Occupational Status

Top figure = Number of respondents

Bottom Figure = % of total in each educational category

Social Class	Poly-tech	Art Acad	Univ-ersity	Sec Schl	Tech Coll	Sem Coll	Fine Arts	Orat-orium	Miss-ing	TOTAL
Peasants	1	0	2	1	1	10	0	0	4	19
	2.8	0	5.2	3.8	3.3	24.0	0	0	36.0	6.9
Unskilled Workers	0	0	1	1	1	2	1	5	0	11
	0	0	2.6	3.8	3.3	4.8	3.8	14.0	0	3.9
Craftsmen	14	10	13	4	13	25	5	20	1	105
	39.2	33.3	33.0	15.4	43.6	61.6	20.2	55.2	9.0	37.8
Non-Manual Workers	5	5	3	8	5	2	10	6	2	46
	14.0	16.5	7.8	30.8	16.5	4.8	38.0	16.8.	19.0	16.6
White-Collar Workers	16	18	20	12	10	2	10	5	4	97
	44.0	50.2	51.4	46.2	33.3	4.8	38.0	14.0	35.5	34.8
TOTAL 36	33	39	26	30	41	26	36	11	278	
	100	100	100	100	100	100	100	100	100	100

as the physically and mentally handicapped. Oratoria thus bear some resemblance to the Protestant inner-city missions. The young people working in them are still engaged in education at secondary schools and colleges.

Table 1 gives the proportion of respondents according to the type of educational establishment, though these figures do not reflect the national distribution of young people between these establishments. Table 2 gives the proportion of respondents coming from homes classified according to father's occupational category, used here as an indicator of social class.

Respondents' worldviews were worked out by means of a questionnaire developed in the Institute for Comparative Religion, at the Abo Akademi, a Swedish speaking university in Finland. The questionnaire uses Likert-type scales. These consist of judgments on value statements ranging from 'strongly approve' to 'strongly disapprove'. The same questionnaire has been used in cross-cultural and inter-religious research in different parts of the world, to date in Europe, the USA, Mexico and Japan (see Holm et al. 1989).

The questionnaire consists of 140 items divided into nine worldview scales, two personality scales, a scale describing relationships to other people, and six further scales describing the relation of the respondent to parents, three for each parent. The least known scales are the 'yuppie' (young, upwardly mobile professionals), expressing a striving for riches and material wealth; the 'ecological', made up of statements about air and soil pollution and nuclear power plants; and the 'neo-Hindu' scale, expressing contemporary forms of acceptance of traditional Hindu thought and practice. Examples of statements drawn from them are provided in Box 1.

All the participants in the study were contacted once, some of them in their university residence, others at their school or place of instruction. Respondents were contacted in groups, in numbers ranging from 12 to 30 persons.

Results and Discussion

The results were not analysed for gender differences because numbers in some educational categories were too small. Means and standard deviations for worldview variables are given in Table 3. The mean here indicates the amount of belief in any given world view expressed across the range of respondents and across particular education categories. In other words, individuals are not the prime units of measurement but the worldviews themselves.

As can be seen, the worldviews differ as to their relative intensity across the whole sample as well as within groups. As a consequence they can be divided into three subcategories:

1) beliefs which have a high degree of acceptance, namely the ecological, the generally religious and the specifically Christian;

Table 3
Intensity of Worldviews Averaged Across the Whole Sample and Across Educational Categories

Maximum Score Possible = 100

Worldview
Categories

Educational Categories
Top figure in each box = Mean (M)
Figures in italics = Standard Deviation (S.D.)

	Total Sample	Poly-techs	Art Acads	Univs Colls	Sec/ Schl	Tech Coll	Semin Colls	Fine Arts	Orat-oria
Atheism	12.33	14.58	19.57	12.71	16.34	16.49	1.01	22.75	6.82
	16.87	*15.86*	*19.36*	*26.21*	*16.91*	*11.46*	*3.33*	*20.22*	*12.76*
Marxism	29.88	27.15	31.59	25.13	33.91	27.93	29.87	32.40	33.21
	14.05	*13.79*	*11.50*	*16.35*	*14.82*	*14.97*	*12.94*	*14.39*	*12.29*
'Yuppie'	33.41	39.03	33.33	40.00	35.87	40.93	20.18	37.69	25.28
Worldview	*18.30*	*19.71*	*15.39*	*18.14*	*20.26*	*16.23*	*14.12*	*17.56*	*14.19*
Magical	44.85	46.00	54.60	47.28	46.60	36.85	42.60	47.12	37.10
Worldview	*13.49*	*16.00*	*11.64*	*14.70*	*11.73*	*15.24*	*12.91*	*12.06*	*9.80*
Neo-Hinduism	42.74	44.21	47.33	47.74	41.51	33.46	39.36	49.60	38.13
	15.07	*13.66*	*14.36*	*14.03*	*17.84*	*18.03*	*12.62*	*14.34*	*11.33*
Mysticism	49.60	48.60	57.47	58.57	49.91	32.40	51.56	47.75	44.90
	17.79	*16.60*	*12.80*	*19.41*	*17.00*	*15.24*	*15.84*	*26.80*	*16.30*
Christian	66.86	61.42	58.67	66.00	60.82	62.57	84.57	54.26	76.85
Worldview	*11.10*	*19.25*	*16.10*	*18.82*	*19.47*	*15.48*	*7.72*	*21.37*	*12.74*
General	68.86	64.93	65.82	70.78	67.55	64.43	73.63	64.82	73.75
Religious	*15.16*	*12.30*	*18.09*	*15.25*	*18.20*	*13.77*	*15.50*	*15.40*	*8.74*
Ecological	78.65	75.89	81.85	80.25	78.69	70.77	83.41	77.11	78.28
Worldview	*12.72*	*11.62*	*13.93*	*14.90*	*11.02*	*11.46*	*11.05*	*11.96*	*12.11*

2) beliefs which have a moderate degree of acceptance, namely the mystical, the magical and the neo-Hindu;
3) beliefs which have a low degree of acceptance, namely the yuppie, the Marxist and the atheist.

Items from the ecological scale received the strongest acceptance in all groups except for the seminarians or trainee priests. Even for seminarians the score was very high and only surpassed by their score for the Christian worldview, a fact which can be explained by their general concern with other-worldly matters. Majority acceptance of the ecological point of view seems to be caused by the fact that ecological consciousness has been raised by the considerable number of publications describing the serious health situation in many regions of Poland. Air pollution caused by heavy industry destroys not only historical monuments, as in Cracow, but also causes a very high rate of allergies in children as well as high incidence of cancer in both the child and adult population. So, the appearance of this concern for the environment could possibly be interpreted as a concern for survival rather than as a genuine alternative to other worldviews.

Christian and general religiosity occupy second and third positions in the hierarchy. They do not differ significantly as to their intensity in the whole sample. The least popular orientations are the atheistic, Marxist and what is termed here yuppie worldviews. It is already clear that among Polish youth there exists a whole spectrum of worldviews and in no case can worldview research be limited to the analysis of different forms of religiosity. New worldview orientations which are not strictly of a religious character are interwoven with religious values. Some of them, namely the belief in magic, neo-Hinduism and concern for the environment, probably have their origins in the specific economic situations of certain professions which have traditionally enjoyed high social status and are now experiencing a reduced standard of living. Marxism and atheism have a political origin in Poland. They are associated with a whole range of actions undertaken by the government in the post-war period to fight Roman Catholicism and convince people that Marxism and atheism should constitute the only foundation for human thought and action, including all institutionalized forms of social and cultural life.

The differences in the popularity of separate worldviews may also be explained by the relation of the respondents' worldviews to various aspects of their parents' influence. This information was obtained by relating respondents' worldviews to their responses to the scales on parental influence (see Box 1 for details of these scales). Table 4 illustrates the differences for each worldview.

Christian and general religiosity correlate positively with almost all aspects of the relationship with parents. The atheistic option negatively correlates in all cases but one. The magical, Marxist, yuppie and ecological worldviews have slender connections with parent-child relationships. Mysticism has a low postive correlation with the Mother's worldview, neo-Hinduism a negative one.

Another aspect of the analysis is revealed by comparing the relative popularity of different worldview orientations according to the type of educational establishment. This can be see by referring back to Table 3. Mystical attitudes appear to be strongest among students from universities and academies of art, and lowest among students from technical colleges. The same pattern can also be observed for the ecological orientation except for the fact that seminarians also report high levels of awareness. The latter also reach the highest level in Christian and general religiosity. By contrast the lowest levels reported are those of the pupils from technical and fine arts schools and colleges. At the same time they score highest in atheistic, Marxist and neo-Hindu attitudes. The groups lowest in atheism are the seminarians and the Oratorium workers, the groups lowest in Marxism the university students, and the lowest in neo-Hinduism are the students from the technical schools and colleges.

Box 1:
Yuppie, Ecological and Neo-Hindu Scales:
Examples of Statements

Yuppie Scale
People have to live with their feet firmly on the ground and think about themselves and how to achieve success.
Money leads to happiness, everything else is self-deception.
A good education is an important prerequisite for a happy and harmonious life.
The more money one has, the greater are the possibilities for happiness.
It is important to strive for both a career and for a good position in society.

Ecological Scale
Humankind has already exterminated many animal species from this planet. If it does not begin to show more respect for nature, it will soon exterminate itself too.
Humankind does not live in balance with nature anymore, and it is of the utmost importance to regain this balance.
World pollution is one of the greatest problems humankind will have to fight.
The development of nuclear power plants constitutes a great danger for mankind.

Neo-Hindu Scale
I have at least ocasionally tried yoga or meditation.
I feel attached to Eastern religions.
I am a vegetarian.
I believe in reincarnation.
People in the West could learn much from Indian Philosophy.

Scale on Influence of the Parents

Relations with mother/father:
My mother [father] used quite strict methods in bringing me up.
During childhood I experienced my mother [father] as a warm and friendly person.

Mother's/Father's worldview:
My mother [father] was an atheist.
My mother [father] was religious.

Transmission of Mother's/Father's worldview:
During my childhood, my mother [father] seldom spoke to me about questions pertaining to an outlook on, or a philosophy of life.
My mother [father] did not succeed very well in transferring her [his] outlook on life to me.

Turning to the magical and yuppie worldviews, one sees that students from the technical schools and colleges are lowest in magic and highest in yuppie attitudes. Seminarians are lowest in the latter category and students of art academies the highest in magic.

Figure 1: Worldview Structure of Polytechnic Students

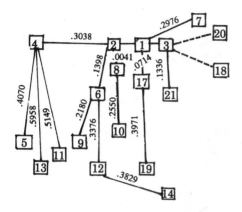

Figure 2: Worldview Structure of Art Academy Students

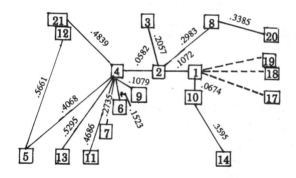

Key to the variables displayed by number in boxes

1 = Age
2 = Mystical Worldview
3 = Ecological Worldview
4 = Christian Worldview
5 = General Religious Worldview
6 = Relations with Others
7 = Self-Concept
8 = Anxiety
9 = Relations with Mother
10 = Relations with Father

11 = Mother's Worldview
12 = Transmission of Mother's Worldv.
13 = Father's Worldview
14 = Transmission of Father's Worldv.
17 = Atheistic Worldview
18 = Marxist Worldview
19 = Yuppie Worldview
20 = Magic Worldview
21 = Neo-Hindu Worldview

Numbers between variables are Pearson correlation coefficients.
The greater the correlation, the shorter the relating line.
---line means no direct correlation but one mediated by another
variable.

Figure 3: Worldview Structure of Secondary and Further Education Students

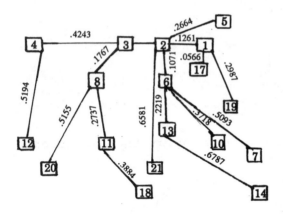

Figure 4: Worldview Structure of Seminary Students

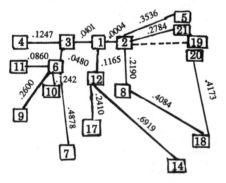

To summarise the results presented in Table 3, one can say that university students represent the most conventional religious worldview with the mystical aspects of it well developed. Mysticism is also well developed in the polytechnic and technical college students.

Students of the academies of art can be characterized by the developed spiritual dimension of their worldview, which at the same time remains unconnected with more traditional forms of religious life.

Students from the seminary and the church-inspired lay group from the Oratoria present a very similar pattern: strong acceptance of traditional forms of religious awareness combined with the most total opposition to atheism and yuppie attitudes of the whole sample. The strongest acceptance of marxist and atheist attitudes was combined with the lowest levels of Christian and general religious attitudes among the young people from the fine arts colleges.

Students from the technical college appear to be the most yuppie-oriented and the least spiritual. This particular result contradicts commonly held views in Poland that people with a technical education appear to be

Table 4. Parental Influence on Respondents' Worldviews

Worldview Category	Relations with Mother	Relations with Father	Mother's Worldview	Father's Worldview	Transm.of Mother's Worldview	Transm.of Father's Worldview
Atheism	-.2395		-.3867	-.3806	-.1999	-.1154
Marxism		-.1066				
"Yuppie" Worldview				-.1991	.0982	
Magical Worldview						-.1546
Neo-Hinduism	-.1118			-.1323	-.1208	
Mysticism	.1477				-.1691	
Christian Worldview	.1946		.3896	.3828	.4844.	.1435
General Relig. Wv	.1270	.2421		.3027	.1301	.1815
Ecologic. Worldview			.1247			

The measure of association is Pearsons's product moment correlation ('r'). Only those correlations are given which are deemed to be significant i.e. where $p < .05$.

generally more religious than those with an education in the humanities. However, this finding could be questionable, as the measures of Christian religiosity from the Abo Akademi consist mainly of statements about religious doctrine and knowledge of the Bible, whereas religious culture in Poland is not really based on knowledge and acceptance of doctrine but mainly on participation in religious rituals (Grzymala-Moszczysnka 1981).

The most interesting part of the research was the exploration of the relationships which appeared between the various worldview orientations, the personality dimensions and students' educational affiliation. These relationships were approached by constructing diagrams based on SPSS dendrograms for each educational category (see Figures 1-4). An analysis of the diagrams makes it clear that worldview structures generally differ between secondary and further education students on the one hand and university students on the other. The university student worldviews seem to be more congruent. Elements contradicting traditional religious orientations are left out. In the college students such contradictory elements are left in. Seminarians and Oratorium workers seem to possess more mature and logically constructed values and beliefs.

Traditional religiosity among secondary and further education students seems to be influenced mainly by the mother but generally remains independent of the relationsip with parents. The religiosity of academy and university students seems to be influenced by both parents.

An acceptance of a mystical orientation appears to be an intermediary factor in the incorporation of new ideologies from contemporary Western European culture into the worldview structure. This explains both why new values of extraneous origin are accepted so slowly within the Polish context, but also explains why the orientation is accepted at all. This is because of the fact that Polish religiosity was never especially directed towards the transcendent as such. It always had and still retains a mainly anthropocentric character. For this reason the mystical aspect of religion has never been predominant. People in general have remained rather unattracted to orientations expressing this aspect of religion.

The research presented here has posed more questions than it has provided ready answers. The results could serve as a source in the generation of new hypotheses which could be tested in order to build a more accurate picture of worldviews in contemporary Poland.

Bibliography

Grzymala-Moszczynska,H 1981 *Postawy mlodziezy akademickiej wobec religii: Struktura i dynamika* (Students' attitudes to religion: structure and dynamic) Krakow.

Holm, N G, Bjorkvist, K, Bergbom, B & Yli-Luoma, P 1989 'Predictors of Worldviews: an attachment-theoretical approach' Paper presented at SSSR Conference, Salt Lake City.

Piwowarski, W 1977 *Religijnosc miejska w warunkach uprzemyslowienia* (Urban religiosity and industrialization) Warsaw.
Strassberg, B 1988 'Changes in Religious Culture in Post War II Poland', *Sociological Analysis* 48: 342-54.

7
The Photograph as a Tool of the Sociology of Religion: a Polish case study

Krzysztof Kosela

In this chapter I will introduce an unusual technique for collecting sociological data in which the main tool is a collection of photographs, illustrating complex real social situations, and then present some results of research using this method, revealing some characteristic features of Polish Catholicism.

The research project took place in August and September 1986 in a major city in northern Poland and was administered to a random sample of 360 industrial workers. Eleven photographs were presented to each interviewee in turn, and various simple questions were asked: What is going on in the photograph? What do these people want? What do they feel? Is this situation typical or unusual? Have you ever been in such a situation?

We found that it was only necessary to ask all these questions for the first few photographs; after that our respondents made their comments without any further prompting. Each interview was recorded on tape.

The data we gathered gave rise to quite a few surprises, not least that the material would be of interest to the sociologist of religion. The photographs illustrated work situations, a demonstration, a political strike, and negotiations in the early 1980s. Only one photograph had an obviously religious content, picturing a Catholic priest preaching at a street demonstration. But this picture provoked extensive comment. This was a consequence of one of the benefits of this technique, exploiting the familiar situation of a group of people gathering to look over and comment on family photographs, a considerable advance on the standard interview, for many people all too reminiscent of a formal police investigation. An average interview with eleven photographs lasted about two hours, but some continued for as long as four hours. Our interviewees turned out to be talkative!

Another surprise was of a methodological character. Although the research was planned to be a replication of surveys of political attitudes made during the 1980s, some of our results turned out to be incompatible with those surveys, and sometimes even contradictory.

Table 1 presents the results of two surveys about the trustworthiness of various institutions, organisations and groups. The first survey, conducted by the Polish Academy of Sciences in 1988, is generally regarded as being more independent than the second survey, carried out by the Government's Social Opinion Centre.

In both these surveys the Catholic church came top as the most trustworthy organisation. Least to be trusted were the illegal Solidarity movement, the Civic Militia and the Polish United Workers Party. But in our research the commentaries on the photograph of the priest preaching to demonstrators from a lorry revealed a strong anti-clericalism which cannot easily be reconciled with the attitudes towards the Church revealed in the Tables.

This prompted reflection on just what our research had revealed. They were of course momentary, tentative, changeable opinions. But I am convinced that underlying this were more profound cognitive structures, or cognitive patterns, idealised mental representations of experiences, shared concepts which help people to interpret everyday situations.

Three examples of cognitive patterns

The notion of religious gathering is an interesting example of such a cognitive pattern. Some of our respondents disapproved of the situation presented in the photograph of the priest on the lorry, saying that mass celebrated in such a context was a profanation. Others disapproved of the militiamen being present, suspecting that they were only waiting for an excuse to break up the religious meeting. Moreover they were wearing hats,

Table 1:
Two Polish Surveys on Attitudes to Institutions

	1: Polish Academy of Science Survey n= 2349 Dec 1987-Jan 1988 *Trustworthiness of institutions.*				2: Social Opinion Centre (governmental) Survey n = 1498 Nov 1987 *Institutions serve interests of society well*			
	yes	no	diff	rank order	yes	no	diff	rank order
Catholic Church	88.1	6.5	81.6	1	78.8	13.0	65.8	1
Parliament	73.0	15.5	57.5	2	70.7	16.7	54.0	3
Army	71.8	15.8	56.0	3	75.0	13.8	61.2	2
People's State Council	63.8	15.2	48.6	4	64.7	18.2	46.5	4
Government	60.5	24.5	36.0	5	63.0	24.0	39.0	5
United Peasants Party	43.5	16.5	27.0	6	46.0	18.6	27.4	6
Democratic Party	40.0	16.7	23.3	7	40.0	19.0	21.0	8
television	48.9	36.4	12.5	8				
mass media					46.3	28.4	17.9	10
Patriotic movement of National Renewal	40.6	29.2	11.4	9	46.3	28.3	18.0	9
new trade unions	34.1	34.2	-0.1	10	47.3	30.5	16.8	11
Civic Militia	38.6	43.9	-5.3	11				
Civic Militia and Ministry of Internal Affairs					53.0	31.5	21.5	7
Polish United Workers Party	37.5	43.8	-6.3	12	44.3	37.0	7.3	12
Solidarity (then illegal)	25.0	43.3	-18.3	13	16.3	45.0	-28.7	13

a profanation in itself at a religious gathering. Another group of respondents disliked such situations because political arguments might arise in the sermon, and they saw politics as something 'dirty'. Thus such celebrations might be spoiled. After all, who were communists in comparison with God and how could their tricks compare with the teaching of Revelation? The two things should not be mixed, they said. The priest was in the wrong.

In such responses, and in the explanations provided to justify them, we can discern the elements of a cognitive pattern on the nature of a religious meeting. It would seem that for many Poles to introduce a priest into any gathering is to introduce a new dimension to the meeting. The gathering gains extra significance as 'heaven comes into contact with earth' and God becomes involved in human affairs. Since priests speak with the higher authority of the divine, participation in such meetings gains a particular significance. In the photograph, whether the exhortations of the priest were taken seriously or not, the meeting was potentially subversive. Another aspect made apparent was the comparison with the past public involvement of the church. Meetings like the one shown might appear to be regarded by some as breaking tradition, and by others as consistent with it.

Another issue is worth mentioning. A major part of our intention in the research was to find out how social life and the public sphere were interpreted by respondents, what they thought was at stake and what they thought people were doing by participating in it. But it was too difficult to ask such questions directly. However, *post factum* reconstruction reveals two opposing sides of the soul of *homo sovieticus*. Respondents tended either to discern the situation depicted in the photograph as a religious meeting, vulnerable to disruption by the militia or by politics, or to identify it as a political meeting. The latter category of people might be labelled *engineers of souls*. If hypnotised they might give very interesting answers to the question - what is social life? For such people it is a place of political struggles where everyone catches as he can. Opponents involved in the game cannot have clean hands. No partner in a political clash could be both strong and innocent. The simple presence of the Catholic church at such a public scene would be sufficient to taint it. For the engineer of souls, people are primitive, an easily-manipulated crowd. Some of our respondents said that the people surrounding the priest would not notice if the priest were replaced by a clown or pop-singer. The only issue at stake in social conflict was power, control and money.

The other interpretation was less clearly discernible. But some people when asked about the nature of social life regarded it as the place where there is a pursuit of truth and brotherhood. Society is not merely the fertiliser of progress in history, society consists of people! Not money, but justice or dignity are what is at stake in social life. This cognitive pattern is less discernible because it is rarely found in a fully articulated form. It is better expressed by more highly-educated people. In the Polish version of this paper I labelled this category, *players in God's playground*. This expression, coined by British historian Norman Davies, soundly describes what some Poles think and feel.

Methodological questions arise as to whether the results of the interviews can be categorised in terms of such cognitive patterns. Psychologists describe several properties of these mental entities. Amongst them is a characteristically hierarchic composition; every cognitive pattern fits as a part of a hierarchical structure and every one has its sub-patterns. Cognitive patterns convey the underlying essence, the 'marrow' of responses. They provide a method of accounting for differing perceptions of the same event - why some respondents regard the priest preaching from the lorry as normal, while for others it is strange and unusual. The technique of photograph analysis makes it possible to detect these more profound mental entities.

Opinions expressed

As has been seen, opinions were also expressed during our interviews on the role of the Church and religion in public life. Public discussion is shaped by the two contenders: on one side the state with its mass media and knowledge of social processes and regularities, and on the other the Catholic church with its strong conviction about what its vocation should be, albeit with less possibility of influencing an audience. Our data allows us to evaluate the effectiveness of persuasion on three controversies in particular. The first is whether the state of religious indifference common in some segments of Polish society is a normal or abnormal state. The second controversial issue concerns the perception of the place of religion in people's lives, and the third, the definition of religious institutions.

It is not difficult for a researcher to reconstruct the standpoints of politicians, but there are problems in identifying the position of the hierarchy of the Catholic Church. The language of bishops' letters and teachings leave room for uncertainty. But a clear indication of the view of the Primate of Poland was provided in an explicit, brief response to a document formulated by the Primate's Social Council. This is an advisory body in which the prestigious and independent intellectuals help the Primate to formulate the Church's position in public discussions. The Social Council had presented its perspective on the Church's public involvement in politics and its attitude toward leftist opposition intelligentsia. The Primate reacted with embarrassment and protest since his advisers seemed to be too modernistic, tolerant and generally passive (Prymas Polski 1988). In a short but firm reprimand the Cardinal delivered a clear definition of the role of the Polish Catholic hierarchy.

The first point of controversy between secular and religious powers concerns secularization. Politicians regarded this as a positive development, and their public relations advisers consider it to be normal, natural and inevitable process. Intellectuals from the Primate's Social Council broadly accepted this analysis, and regarded religious indifference and agnosticism as long-term feature of social life which would have to be tolerated. The Primate responded strongly that his advisers were totally wrong. The Church could not accept a view of man devoid of divinity, and could not abandon its efforts to reverse this unnatural condition. Opinions expressed during our interviews show that our respondents, and presumably most adult Poles, make a compromise. They do not share the missionary endeavour of their first shepherd, but they display their religious indifference reluctantly. When asked about their denomination in Torun in 1982, 96% of the sample answered that they were Roman Catholics. Surprisingly perhaps, a smaller proportion regarded themselves as believers.

The second controversy concerns the role of religion and the nature of the religious life. Politicians recognise that the Catholic Church is a significant political factor in Poland but they also refer to the weakness of religion as an agency for promoting public and personal morality. The minimal effectiveness of Catholic crusades against alcoholism was pointed out with satisfaction by government spokesmen. Religion was considered as a disease. Politicians would prefer it to be an uninfectious disease with no symptoms. Religion for them, was the affair of the private individual. But the Primate argued that religion was not a private affair as the communists used to suggest, but rather that people's personal affairs had public, that is to say social, consequences. Our respondents were not sufficiently subtle to distinguish private from personal affairs. What they immediately noticed and willingly reported were the functions of religion and the Church for individuals and for such abstract qualities as ethical values. What is interesting is that while the Primate insisted that the church could not abandon its attempt to shape social and public reality, the responses of our interviewees yielded nothing that resembled the social teaching of the Catholic church.

There is one more controversial issue. It deals with the effectiveness of political and religious authorities in their attempt to influence society. This is the controversy concerning the definition of the Church. Politicians claim that the Church is a particular organisation, but believers are nothing more than a category of people who happen to share a characteristic religious identification. The Church's definition states that it is a mystical body. The fact of baptism incorporates people within this body, and nothing, or almost nothing, can separate them from the Church. The Primate said that even communist activists who are not cynics feel reverence for the Church and are indeed Catholics. It is interesting that our interviewees turned out to be more experienced and innovative than the Primate. Naturally some of them agreed with the politicians, while it was also evident that for some the Church shapes people rather than that believers create the Church. But the comments on our photographs revealed an awareness that even priests and bishops apparently failed to perceive, that people, when gathered for special religious occasions felt that they constitute something more than the mystical entity alluded to by the Primate: a vibrant and caring community who shared each others' feelings and sentiments. Such statements would not sound so genuine when written as replies on questionnaire forms, but they gain an authenticity when reported as personal recollections stimulated by photographs.

Our respondents here demonstrated a striking independence. In the face of the competing efforts of Church and state to influence society, they did not echo the sentiments of the addresses delivered from tribunes or pulpits.

Advantages and disadvantages of the technique

The technique of using photographs has therefore some definite advantages. In this chapter I have argued that it allowed us to identify profound psychic entities which are examples of cognitive patterns. It has also proved to be a potent tool in analysing opinions as they are revealed in the conversations prompted by the photographs. A further possible application, not developed further here, is to infer people's attitudes on the basis of what they do not express. For example, no criticism of sacerdotalism was expressed in the interviews.

Our findings contribute towards an understanding of the strange split within Polish Catholic identification. On the one hand there is a clearly manifested denominational identification, but a private religious identification is rarely present in Polish minds. Poles distance themselves from the Church when their personal conduct is considered and identify with their Church when political need emerges.

The photographic technique does have disadvantages, of course. The presentation of photographs opens up pandora's box. The researcher is overwhelmed by an abundance of information and has scarcely any control over the elements he has released. A questionnaire item resembles a key that opens only one intended door. Photographs in the hands of respondents are skeleton keys that open unintended as well as intended doors. The co-operation of researchers and photographers will be necessary to refine these techniques.

Bibliography

Collier, J, 1967, *Visual Anthropology: Photography as a Research Method*, New York: Holt, Rinehart and Winston.

Kosela, K, forthcoming: 'Interpretacja fotografil-krok ku socjologil' wizualnej. in *Kultura i Spoleczenstwo*.

Prymas Polski 1988: 'Poszanowanie swiatopogladow w panstwie i spoleczenstwie' z dnia 6 czerwca.

Trzebinski J, 1985   'Rola systemow poznawczych w zachowanioach spolecznych', in M Lewicka, ed, *Psychologia postrzegania spolecznego*. Warszawa: KiW .

8
Re-Membering Hare Krishna: Patterns of Disaffiliation and Re-entry

E.Burke Rochford, Jr.

Over the past two decades research on new religious movements has produced considerable empirical and theoretical insight into the dynamics of recruitment and participation in religious groups and movements (Barker 1986; Rambo 1980; Snow and Machalek 1984). More recently investigators have also begun to explore the range of factors which influence defection from new religious movements (Bromley 1988; Jacobs 1984, 1987; Rochford 1989; Skonovd 1981, 1983; Wright 1983b, 1984, 1988). Despite the rather impressive accumulation of findings addressing issues of membership in new religions, little research has focused on the process of disaffiliation and subsequent re-entry, or what I refer to here as *re-membering* (but see Beckford 1985:169-171). Moreover, as Roozen has suggested, questions of disengagement and re-entry have received relatively little attention from scholars of conventional faiths as well (1980:431).

> Most studies of religious disengagement and disaffiliation stop at the point of defection giving the impression that disengagement represents a permanent state. Such an impression is heightened by the lack of any substantive body of research on the 'rechurching' of church dropouts. But, is it true that 'once a dropout always a dropout'? Of course not! But, beyond observing that at least some dropouts return to active church involvement, existing research has precious little to say on the topic (1980:431).

Roozen (1980:427) estimates that 46% of the U.S. population drops out of active church participation at some point in their lifetime. Yet for most church drop-outs disengagement is only temporary. As many as 80% of all church dropouts eventually return to active involvement. The younger the individual at the point of disengagement the greater the probability that they will return to their previous religious organization. Albrecht *et al.*, (1988:65) estimate that eight out of ten Mormons disengage from the church at some point during their lives. Yet by age 65, 'a majority of those who do will eventually return to activity and begin to attend worship services or will report that their religious beliefs have taken on renewed importance' (1988:66; also see Hoge 1981).

Clearly, questions of re-entry have practical importance for conventional and unconventional religious faiths. Moreover, the process of disaffiliation and re-membering raises a number of theoretical questions regarding religious involvement and the relationship between membership on the one hand and conversion on the other. The present study explores the dynamics of adherent withdrawal from, and re-membering with, the International Society for Krishna Consciousness (ISKCON). Questions of re-entry have special relevance for the conflict surrounding cults. It has often been argued by anti-cultists that deprogramming and litigation directed toward extraction of cult members is necessary because the latter lack individual free will and/or any reasonable opportunity to weigh the options of staying or leaving (Rochford et al. 1989). Because the present research documents a pattern of voluntary disaffiliation and subsequent re-entry among a portion of ISKCON's membership, it challenges anti-cult views.

I first explore various theoretical treatments of voluntary disengagement and re-entry. Empirically, I examine the influence of a range of social psychological and structural/organizational factors on disaffiliation from ISKCON. With respect to the question of re-entry, I link ex-members' life situations in the conventional society to decisions to re-member ISKCON. The findings presented suggest that disengagement remains an uncertain and ambiguous transition for many who withdraw from communally organized and exclusive religious organizations like ISKCON. Whether defector status is actually realized appears to be influenced more by ex-members' post-involvement activities than changes in faith and commitment predating decisions to exit. I argue that re-membering ISKCON is a strategic option for leavers - most of whom retain their faith in Krishna Consciousness, if not commitment to ISKCON - when their transition into the conventional society proves unsuccessful.

Predictors of Voluntary Disaffiliation and Re-entry

With the decline of new religious movements there has been a corresponding shift in the research agenda of scholars studying these groups. The past several years has produced dozens of studies of individual, and to a lesser degree, collective forms of disengagement i.e. group defection and schism (but see Rochford 1989). As Wright's (1988) recent review article suggests much of the work on defection has borrowed and adapted concepts and theoretical models previously used to account for membership in new religious movements. If people join new religions because their values and beliefs are aligned with those of a particular religious movement, or such an alignment is established during recruitment, then defection logically involves a breakdown in that crucial linkage. If individuals undergo conversion as part of joining, then they necessarily undergo a reverse process of 'deconversion' as part of disaffiliating from a new religious group (Jacobs 1984, 1987; Skonovd 1979). From such a framework, defection is fundamentally a process of cognitive reorganization (Skonovd 1979).

Studies of defection have thus assumed that those who voluntarily withdraw from new religions hold unique attitudes and cognitive orientations that distinguish them from committed members. If defectors report declining commitment toward the group's religious doctrine and/or practices then we speak of their having 'fallen from the faith' as an explanation for disengagement (Brinkerhoff and Burke 1980; Bromley 1988).

Researchers employing a conventional social psychological approach have also sought to incorporate organizational and structural factors into their theories of defection (Wright 1988). Factors influencing individual decisions to disaffiliate include: the influence of leader decisions and abuses of power (Jacobs 1984, 1987; Wright 1983a), changes in organizational policies (Ebaugh 1977; Ofshe 1980; Rochford 1985: 209-210; 1989; Wallis 1982: 92-93), organizational decline and disintegration (Balch and Cohig 1985; Hall 1987; Rochford 1985), a weakening of internal social bonds (Albrecht et al. 1988: 68; Downton 1979: 218; Wright 1986) and countervailing external ties with friends and family (Barker 1988:181; Galanter 1980:1578; Wright and Piper 1986). Although structural and organizational factors have been addressed in recent work on defection they have been largely reduced to social psychological influences. Which is to say, structural/organizational considerations are seen as important only in as much as they create cognitive dissonance problems for the soon-to-be ex-member (Rochford 1989). The literature on defection from new religions is skewed toward a consideration of what Mauss (1969) refers to as the intellectual dimension of defection.

Because studies of disengagement from new religious groups normally stop at the point of departure, defection becomes frozen in time (Beckford 1985: 138) rather than a role transition requiring ongoing 'ideological work' (see Berger 1981; Rochford 1989) and lifestyle adjustments. Moreover, this static, nonprocessual view of defection gives the impression that withdrawal is largely accomplished prior to exiting; that soon-to-be ex-members weight the costs and benefits associated with continued membership and rationally decide to re-enter the conventional society. To the extent that studies have gone beyond the point of withdrawal they have focused largely on members who have been involuntarily extracted from new religions. These latter studies have focused on various forms of exit counselling and the role played by the anti-cult movement in 'resocializing' ex-members into conventional roles, lifestyles and worldviews (Lewis 1986; Solomon 1981).

Also overlooked in most studies of defection is the fact that some ex-members consciously attempt to hold on to their unconventional beliefs (see Beckford 1985: 169; Rochford 1985: 87-122; 1989). In disaffiliating they have not turned their backs on their faith, but rather a religious organization they deem unworthy of their membership. Therefore, in the same way 'conversion and recruitment are not synonyms' (Beckford 1985: 174) neither are deconversion and defection.

Richardson's (1978, 1980) notion of 'conversion careers' allows us to take a more dynamic view of withdrawal. Such a framework allows for viewing defection as potentially little more than a temporary oscillation in a believer's spiritual development. Surprisingly, scholars of new religions have generally failed to focus empirically on the dynamics of conversion careers, other than to note that some ex-members join other new or traditional religious groups and organizations. Jacobs (1987) for example found that 50 percent of the defectors in her sample had subsequently become affiliated with a different religious group. Similarly, Wright (1987: 53) reports that 53% of the defectors he studied ultimately became members of fundamentalist or evangelical churches (on Hutterite defection and conversion to evangelical Protestantism see Peter et al. 1982). Here I am going to concentrate on defectors whose conversion career includes returning or re-membering, rather than switching (Stark and Glock 1968; Newport 1979).

Although there is little empirical evidence identifying the factors underlying re-membering with new religions, four processes can be derived from the literature: (1) a renewal of faith in the group's religious beliefs, religious practices, and/or lifestyle (Albrecht et al 1988: 66; Beckford 1985: 169; Rauff 1979: 160); (2) commitment and dedication to the group's charismatic/spiritual leader (Jacobs 1987); (3) interpersonal ties and feelings of group solidarity (Beckford 1985: 169; Rauff 1979: 161); (4) personal crisis (Rauff 1979: 168).

Methods and Data

Most studies have sought to identify the determinants of defection by asking ex-members to report on their reasons for disaffiliation. These ex-member accounts are then treated as unique, if not objective, in that it is assumed that those who remain within the movement are not 'afflicted' with similar problems and concerns. Unfortunately, one is left to wonder

Table 1
Length of Time Disengaged from ISKCON

Length of Time	N	(%)
Less than two weeks	17	38%
2 weeks - 3 months	14	31%
3 months - 1 year	5	11%
1 year - 5 years	9	20%
Total	45	100%

whether there are indeed differences in the attitudes and life experiences of defectors and those who continue their membership. Surely many, if not most, followers of new religious movements experience occasional personal and spiritual crises which challenge their faith and commitment. The question that needs answering is, why do some members with 'crises' withdraw while others remain?

Data for the present paper were derived from a larger study of recruitment and membership in the Hare Krishna movement (Rochford 1982, 1985). The data reported were derived from a questionnaire completed by 214 ISKCON members in six communities in the United States in 1980. Among a variety of other questions, respondents were asked whether they had encountered any spiritual or personal 'crises' during their time in ISKCON which had either led them to consider disengaging, or if they had actually left for a period of time. Nearly half (46%) of my devotee respondents reported having 'crises' which threatened their membership in ISKCON. Moreover, one in five (N=45) reported 'blooping' (ISKCON term for defection) at some point during their membership in ISKCON.

Respondents experiencing crises of faith and commitment, whether remaining in ISKCON, or having left for a period of time, were asked to report on the source or sources of their disillusionment. Moreover, those who actually disengaged were asked to report on how long they had been away from ISKCON before rejoining, where they had lived, what they had done during this period, as well as their reasons for re-membering ISKCON. Table 1 indicates the length of time that those re-membering were actually disengaged from ISKCON. The length of time reported varies from as little as a few hours to five years. I have counted respondents as leavers if they defined their departure from ISKCON as 'blooping'. While some may argue that those departing for hours or days should not be properly viewed as having disaffiliated, I would only point out that their intention upon leaving was to give up their membership in ISKCON; that they changed their mind and re-entered after a short period is itself a question worthy of empirical consideration and analysis.

In comparing the backgrounds and demographic profiles of leavers, with other ISKCON members who either experienced crises and remained, or reported no crises, I found little that distinguished between the three groups. Table 2 compares the social backgrounds of leavers and members suffering crises but staying on with ISKCON. Other comparisons having theoretical relevance are reported below.

Findings and Discussion

Findings in Table 3 report the reasons given by leavers and stayers for their 'crises' of faith and commitment. These data allow for comparative analysis of members who have experienced crises of commitment and faith, and have disengaged, with those who have experienced crises but remained

Table 2
Background Comparisons Between Leavers and Stayers

Background Variable	Leavers (N=45)	Stayers (N=54)	
A. Demographic Data			
Length of ISKCON membership	4.2	3.6	
(1) < 1 yr. (2) 1-2 yrs.(3) 2-4 yrs. (4) 4-5 yrs. (5) > 5 yrs.			
Age when joined ISKCON	21.9	21.9	
Married prior to ISKCON (% yes)	24%	13%	
B. Religious Involvement Growing Up			
Family stressed religion (1.Yes 2. No)	1.60	1.48	
How often attend religious services with family			
(1) rarely (2) < 1/mo. (3) 1-2/mo (4) weekly (5) > 1/wk.	3.55	2.96	
C. Previous Movement Involvements, Self-Help			
Political movements	18%	20%	
Anti-war movement	33%	27%	
Counterculture	56%	43%	
Religious movements	22%	21%	
Therapy	29%	9%	**
Total number of prior movement involvements	1.64	1.48	
D. Life Situation Immediately Prior To Joining ISKCON			
Feeling discouraged, anxious about my life	51%	63%	
Neither working nor attending school	40%	23%	
Time living on street	42%	30%	
Looking for new friends and			
social contacts	22%	34%	
Using drugs (% yes)	87%	89%	
E. Selected Reasons for Joining ISKCON			
Life was going nowhere; wanted to			
explore other lifestyles	51%	64%	
ISKCON offered a secure way of life	36%	53%	
Seeking spiritual knowledge	90%	82%	

** $p < .01$

within ISKCON. While one might logically assume that there would be telling differences between the two groups, in fact, little distinguishes them. Leavers more often than stayers reported breaking, or desiring to break, the movement's regulative principles (e.g. prohibitions against sexual involvement) as a challenge to their membership in ISKCON. However, stayers expressed somewhat more displeasure toward ISKCON's book distribution policies than leavers. Of greatest theoretical significance is the relatively small number of leavers and stayers who reported a loss of faith in Krishna Consciousness as the basis of their commitment problems. This

Table 3
Reasons Cited by Leavers and Stayers for
Commitment Crisis

Reasons	Leavers (N=45)		Stayers (N=54)	
A. Faith and Religious Practice				
1. Lost faith, began to doubt Krishna Consciousness	11%	(9)	10%	(13)
2. Breaking or desire to break regulative principles	30%	(24)	24%	(30)
B. Organizational Influences				
1. Differences with local ISKCON authorities	17%	(14)	17%	(21)
2. Dissatisfaction with ISKCON policies	12%	(10)	8%	(10)
3. ISKCON's book distribution policies/practices	5%	(4)	11%	(14)
4. Lack of adequate financial support from ISKCON	4%	(3)	6%	(7)
5. Work related problems within ISKCON	11%	(9)	14%	(18)
C. Interpersonal Ties/Relations				
1. Family/Marital problems	10%	(8)	10%	(13)
Total	(100%)	(81)	(100%)	(126)

Some respondents provided more than one reason to account for their crisis of commitment.

suggests that approaches to defection that emphasize 'falling from the faith' and 'deconversion' do not adequately account for withdrawal from ISKCON, at least not for leavers who ultimately rejoin. In sum, the data in Table 3 reveal no significant differences between leavers and stayers with regard to the factors which adversely influenced their faith and commitment, though one must accept that the absence of a control group of permanent leavers does not permit any stronger conclusion than this. However Barker (1988: 181) reports that she found little or no statistical differences to distinguish between the backgrounds of apostates and 'continuers' in her sample of Unification Church members.

Table 4 provides findings which go beyond the personal accounts of stayers and leavers. The data reported attempt to assess the influence of member integration, external countervailing ties, and the availability of members to make the transition back into the conventional society. One might reasonably expect that leavers would be less integrated into ISKCON (push factor), have more interpersonal contacts outside of the movement (pull factor), and be available to undertake a major role transition back into the conventional society (i.e. with more education, and few movement ties and constraints).

Although the findings indicated in Table 4 are all in the direction of the expected relationships - leavers are less well integrated into ISKCON, have

Table 4
Measures of Member Integration, Countervailing Ties, and Structural Availability

Measures	Leavers (N=45)	Stayers (N=54)
A. *Movement Integration*		
1. Total number of ISKCON communities resided in	2.6	2.0**
2. Divorced while ISKCON member (% yes)	18%	9%
3. Kin (i.e., brothers, sisters) ISKCON members	0	13%
B. *External Countervailing Ties and Relationships.* (a.)		
1. Maintain non-ISKCON member contacts (% yes)	27%	23%
2. Number of non-ISKCON friends contacted	.76	.55
3. Average number of contacts monthly	1.12	.64
4. When joined, parents unfavourable toward ISKCON	55%	47%
C. *Structurally Available for Defection*		
1. College degree (% yes)	22%	15%
2. Sex (% Male)	64%	43%*
3 Males without children (b.)	83%	75%
4. Females without children	56%	59%

* p<.05. **p<.01.

ªIt is unclear whether measures (B. 1-3) can be viewed as predictors of leave-taking or outcomes of disengagement. The findings reported deal with non-devotee contacts at the time the questionnaire was administered, not contacts held prior to leavers actually withdrawing from ISKCON. I include these measures because other researchers (see Wright 1986; Wright and Piper 1986) have made use of similar retrospective reports from defectors, and the data reported are thus useful for comparative purposes.

ᵇThese data may overstate whether leavers and stayers had children at the time they actually left ISKCON, or contemplated doing so. It is possible that leavers had children only after returning to ISKCON. Stayers may also have had children after their crisis of faith and commitment had passed.

more external contacts with friends and parents, and face fewer barriers impeding their transition into the conventional society - the differences between leavers and stayers are generally minimal. The only significant difference between leavers and stayers is that the former are more likely to be male, and to have moved around between ISKCON communities.

Taken as a whole, the findings presented in Tables 3 and 4 provide little evidence to distinguish between stayers and leavers. Only being male, and less integrated into ISKCON, distinguishes leavers from stayers. While these latter findings suggest a structural analysis, the evidence is too limited and inconclusive to pursue reasonably such a theoretical course. Rather, it seems that the findings are more in keeping with Beckford's observation that there often is an 'indeterminacy and confused character' (1985:142) associated with members' withdrawing from new religious movements. This confusion and uncertainty may logically be even greater for those ex-members who ultimately rejoin their previous religious group. As one young woman who left ISKCON, only to rejoin a year later explained:

> The reason I left was more like a whimsical thing. It wasn't that I was in maya (breaking the principles). I hadn't even been thinking about it until it happened really. It was a very whimsical decision. It wasn't even like I wanted to leave. I just thought I would, to see what it was like.... I never could pinpoint a reason why I did it except that I must have had some material desires that I wanted to cultivate. That was the only logical explanation I could find.

It would seem that the search for statistical probabilities in the backgrounds and decision making of leavers ultimately tells us little about disengagement as a social or interactional accomplishment (Beckford 1985:139).

Profiles of Ex-Member Adaptation

If we are left largely unable to account for defection by isolating what is unique about 'defector's thoughts, feelings, and actions' (Beckford 1985:142) within ISKCON, then it seems reasonable to expand our inquiry out into the society into which ex-members go. Following the lead of role theory, at least within the symbolic interactionist tradition, I assume that roles, and role transitions, are interactional achievements. As such, leaving does not make a defector. Leaving is a behavioral act; to become a defector is a problematic role transition, which may or may not be attained by those who withdraw from religious or secular movements.

If we view defector status as an interactional accomplishment then we must consider the ways in which leavers seek, or perhaps do not seek, to realize this identity through a process of emergent role-passage (see Bromley and Shupe 1986; Beckford 1985:142; San Giovanni 1978). In the present case, of course, the ex-members under investigation ultimately fail to become defectors. Such a group of leavers is empirically and theoretically of interest precisely because their experience points to the problematic character of being 'recruited back into conventional social networks' (Lewis and Bromley 1987:511) and ultimately to the dominant worldview.

Table 5 reports on where those withdrawing from ISKCON went upon leaving. Over half (56%) took up residence with their parents. Those ex-members who were married and/or had children were more likely to have moved into an apartment or house after their departure from ISKCON, sometimes after a period of residing with parents. A few moved in with non-devotee friends while some either took up residence with other former ISKCON members, or spent time travelling and living on the road.

Table 6 indicates that the majority of the leavers did not become involved, or only became marginally involved, in conventional networks and

Table 5
Residence Upon Leaving ISKCON

Residence	N	(%)
Parents, relatives	23	56%
Non-Devotee Friends	3	7%
On own (i.e., house, apartment)	8	20%
Other ex-ISKCON members	2	5%
On the street/travelling	5	12%
Total	(41)	(100%)

activities (i.e. employment and school). Most reported spending their time sleeping, visiting with parents and siblings, continuing to read ISKCON's religious texts, and chanting Hare Krishna. While one-third (N=14) specifically mentioned continuing to keep up their religious practice (e.g. chanting) only two freely admitted to breaking ISKCON's regulative principles (e.g. consumption of drugs, sexual affairs). Fully, two-thirds of those leaving ISKCON made little or no attempt to pursue conventional careers (e.g. employment and/or school) or otherwise reestablish social network ties beyond their immediate family.

Considering the findings reported in Tables 5 and 6, it seems that the majority of leavers remained isolated and essentially uninvolved in the conventional society. The following statements by two leavers underscore this point:

Table 6
Activities During Defection Period

Activity	N	(%)
Worked	8	20%
Attended school	5	13%
Visited with parents and friends	6	15%
Travelled	4	10%
Vacationed,"hung-out," "nothing"	16	40%
Tried to start a schismatic Hare Krishna group	1	3%
Total	40	(101%)

Thankfully, my parents were helpful and understanding - they took care of me until I got back on my feet. I want to stress that never at any time did I consider that being in Krishna Consciousness was the cause of my problems... When I lived with my parents I did not become involved in material life. I lived like a recluse. I would also follow the regulative principles, chant 16 rounds daily, and do some devotional service at home.

We maintained a Vedic lifestyle on our own, excluding all visitors except those interested in the philosophy; worked and kept to ourselves except for a few friends.

Table 7
Reasons Given for Decision to Re-member ISKCON

Reasons	N	(%)
Faith in Krishna	3	6%
Commitment to the philosophy of Krishna Consciousness	6	12%
Dedication to my spiritual master	7	14%
Nothing to offer or enjoy in the outside material society	14	29%
Nothing more satisfying or meaningful than spiritual life	5	10%
Interpersonal ties to ISKCON members	7	14%
Preaching efforts of ISKCON members	4	8%
Other reasons	3	6%
Total	49	99%

Four of the forty-five respondents provided two reasons for re-membering with ISKCON

Re-Membering ISKCON

Table 7 reports on the reasons given by leavers for re-membering ISKCON. A near equal number rejoined because of their negative experiences in the conventional society, or because of factors more directly tied to their religious faith.

One-third accounted for their decision by suggesting they had found nothing attractive to offer in the conventional society and/or that they had come to realize there was nothing more meaningful and satisfying than spiritual life. Consider the words of one woman who left ISKCON for a year-and-a-half with her son, before rejoining.

Now that I have become fed up with the system and have seen that I can work so very hard to earn a nice salary only to have over half taken out by Uncle Sam before I see my paycheck, I would prefer to work harder for Krsna and not worry about money at all. Earning a salary in today's world is a great sham; we have a cheating government. It is because of this outside influence that I have become very much committed to ISKCON. I have so little respect for the government that I will never go back to work for it again if I have to starve. But that can not happen when Krsna is taking care of us; as long as we continue to serve Him.

But while some former members rejoined because of their alienation from conventional society most did so because they had not actively sought to gain any level of integration (as documented in Table 5). They essentially found themselves unable, or unwilling, to become involved in conventional networks or roles. As the following statements suggest, some leavers rejoined ISKCON to overcome their state of liminality (Turner 1977):

After three weeks living at my father's house, sleeping, reading, and eating watermelon, I returned. I just had no inspiration to make friends with anyone and my father made fun of the devotees constantly.

I returned to ISKCON because there is nothing else worthwhile. I'd already tried it all. I was just miserable in the material world and could see that my life had no meaning without devotional service. Karmie [non-devotee] life sickened me, I was bored.

Although few leavers exited ISKCON because of a loss of faith in Krishna Consciousness many chose to return because of the strength of their belief, and commitment to their spiritual master:

I returned [to ISKCON] because I was feeling guilty about not keeping my vows to my spiritual master. Although I broke all the principles, watched television, looked for work, saw old friends, and fried out [took drugs], I never forgot the purport of the philosophy, but consciously acted in deference to it.

I finally realized after a week at my mother's house the importance of Srila Prabhupada's kindness. How could I be so ungrateful? How could I give up living for the Absolute Truth he was giving?

Still others re-membering ISKCON did so because of ties with other ISKCON members. One in five mentioned that they had maintained contact with ISKCON friends and that these relationships were instrumental to their return. These relationships served social as well as ideological functions in decisions to rejoin:

A devotee phoned and preached to me. When I went to visit all the devotees overwhelmed me with their kindness and purity.

Conclusions

The findings reported suggest that those exiting ISKCON (only to re-member sometime later) share many of the same characteristics as those who face crises of faith and commitment but remain within ISKCON. Reasons cited by leavers and stayers for their individual crises were virtually the same. Although leavers appear less integrated into the movement, and have somewhat more external countervailing ties and relationships, these differences for the most part are statistically weak and insignificant. The only significant finding is that males (especially those without children) are more likely to exit ISKCON in the face of crises of faith and commitment than are woman (see Peter et al. 1982:328, on gender and marital status as factors in defection from the Hutterites).

It appears that re-entry into ISKCON - and thereby failure in gaining status as a defector - is largely a function of two interrelated factors. Firstly the majority of those exiting ISKCON retained their status as converts. Only about one in ten who left did so because of a crisis of faith. While many did depart because they were either breaking ISKCON's lifestyle restrictions, or desired to do so, they continued to hold on to their Krishna conscious beliefs.

Secondly in retaining their Krishna conscious worldview upon departing from ISKCON leavers found themselves in a position of needing to bridge their Krishna beliefs and religious practices with the role demands and expectations of the conventional society (see Snow et al. 1986; Rochford 1989, on frame alignment and cognitive bridge-work). As we have seen, this effort proved unsuccessful, either because it failed in practice, or because ex-members strategically avoided becoming drawn into the conventional society (i.e. undertook strategies of isolation). It was this failure to come to terms with living in the conventional society while continuing to practice their unconventional religious beliefs which resulted in leavers re-membering ISKCON. In a real sense, the leavers studied were unable, or unwilling, to complete the role transition from member to defector. Between two social worlds they could not bridge, they rejoined ISKCON, in some cases, despite serious reservations about ISKCON's policies and leadership.

Bibliography

Albrecht, S, Cornwall, M, Cunningham, P 1988   'Religious leave-taking: Disengagement and disaffiliation among Mormons', in Bromley, D (Ed), *Falling from the Faith: Causes and Consequences of Religious Apostasy*, Newbury Park, CA: Sage: 62-80.

Balch, R and Cohig J 1985 'The magic kingdom: A story of Armageddon in utopia', paper presented at the annual meetings of the Society for the Scientific Study of Religion, Savannah, GA.

Barker, E 1986 'Religious movements: Cult and anti-cult since Jonestown', *Annual Review of Sociology* 12: 329-46.

Barker, E 1988 'Defection from the Unification Church: Some Statistics and Distinctions', in Bromley, D (Ed), *Falling from the Faith: Causes and Consequences of Religious Apostasy*, Newbury Park, CA: Sage: 166-184

Beckford, J 1985 *Cult Controversies: The Societal Response to New Religious Movements*, New York: Tavistock.

Berger, B 1981 *The Survival of a Counterculture*, Berkeley: University of California Press.

Brinkerhoff, M and Burke, K 1980 'Disaffiliation: Some notes on 'falling from the faith', *Sociological Analysis* 41: 41-54.

Bromley, D (Ed) 1988 *Falling From the Faith, Causes and Consequences of Religious Apostasy*, Newbury Park, CA: Sage.

Bromley, D and Shupe, A 1986 'Affiliation and disaffiliation: A role theory interpretation of joining and leaving new religious movements', presented at the annual meetings of the Association of the Sociology of Religion, San Antonio, TX.

Downton, J 1979 *Sacred Journeys: The Conversion of Young People to Divine Light Mission*, New York: Columbia University Press.

Ebaugh, H 1977 *Out of the Cloister: A Study of Organizational Dilemmas*, Austin: University of Texas Press.

Galanter, M 1980 'Psychological induction into the large group: Findings from a modern religious sect', *American Journal of Psychiatry* 137: 1574-9.

Hall, J 1987 *Gone from the Promised Land: Jonestown in American Cultural History*, New Brunswick, NJ: Transaction.

Hoge, D. 1981 *Converts, Dropouts, Returnees: A Study of Religious Change Among Catholics*, New York: Pilgrim Press.

Jacobs, J 1984 'The economy of love in religious commitment: The deconversion of women from nontraditional religious movements', *Journal for the Scientific Study of Religion* 23: 155-71

Jacobs, J 1987 'Deconversion from religious movements: An analysis of charismatic bonding and spiritual commitment', *Journal for the Scientific Study of Religion* 26: 294-308.

Lewis, J 1986 'Reconstructing the cult experience: Post-involvement attitudes as a function of mode of exit and post-involvement socialization', *Sociological Analysis* 47: 151-59.

Lewis, J and Bromley, D 1987 'The cult withdrawal syndrome: A case study of misattribution of cause', *Journal for the Scientific Study of Religion* 26: 508-22.

Mauss, A 1969 'Dimensions of religious defection', *Review of Religious Research* 10: 128-135.

Newport, F 1979 'The religious switcher in the United States', *American Sociological Review* 44: 528-552.

Ofshe, R 1980 'The social development of the Synanon Cult', *Sociological Analysis* 41(2): 109-127.

Peter, K, Boldt, E, Palmer, S, Whitaker,I and Roberts, L 1982 'The dynamics of religious defection among Hutterites', *Journal for the Scientific Study of Religion* 21(4): 327-337.

Rambo, L 1982 'Bibliography: Current research on religious conversion', *Religious Studies Review* 8: 146-59.

Rauff, E 1979 *Why People Join the Church*, New York: Pilgrim Press.

Richardson, J 1978 *Conversion Careers*, Beverly Hills, CA: Sage.

Richardson, J 1980 'Conversion Careers', *Society* 17: 47-50.

Rochford, E B Jr 1982 'Recruitment strategies, ideology, and organization in the Hare Krishna movement', *Social Problems* 29: 399-410.

Rochford, E B Jr 1985 *Hare Krishna in America*, New Brunswick, NJ: Rutgers University Press.

Rochford, E B, Jr 1989 'Factionalism, group defection, and schism in the Hare Krishna movement', *Journal for the Scientific Study of Religion* 28(2): 162-79.

Rochford, E B, Jr, Purvis, S and Eastman, N 1989 'New religions, mental health and social control', in Lynn, M and Moberg, D (Eds), *Research in the Social Scientific Study of Religion*, Vol. 1, Greenwich, Conn.: JAI Press

Roozen, D 1980 'Church Dropouts: Changing patterns of disengagement and re-entry', *Review of Religious Research* 21(4): 427-450.

San Giovanni, L 1978 *Ex-Nuns: A Study of Emergent Role Passage*, Norwood, NJ: Ablex.

Skonovd, L 1979 'Becoming an apostate: A model of religious defection', presented at the annual meetings of the Pacific Sociological Association, Anaheim.

Skonovd, L 1981 'Apostasy: The process of defection from religious totalism', Ph.D. dissertation, Ann Arbor, Michigan: University Microfilms International.

Skonovd, L 1983 'Leaving the cultic religious milieu', in Bromley, D and Richardson, J (Eds), *The Brainwashing/Deprogramming Controversy* New York: The Edwin Mellen Press: 91-103.

Snow, D, and Machalek, R 1984 'The sociology of conversion', in Turner, R and Short, J (Eds), *Annual Review of Sociology*, Palo Alto, CA: Annual Reviews Inc: 167-90.

Snow, D E, Rochford, B Jr, Worden, S and Benford, R 1986 'Frame alignment processes, micromobilization, and movement participation', *American Sociological Review* 51: 464-81.

Solomon, T 1981 'Integrating the 'Moonie' experience: A survey of ex-members of the Unification Church', in Robbins, T and Anthony, D (Eds), *In Gods We Trust: New Patterns of Religious Pluralism in America*, New Brunswick, NJ: Transaction: 275-296.

Stark, R and Glock, C 1968 *American Piety: The Nature of Religious Commitment*, Berkeley: University of California Press.

Turner, V 1977 *The Ritual Process*, Ithaca, NY: Cornell University Press.

Wallis, R 1982 *Millennialism and Charisma*, Belfast: The Queen's University.

Wright, S 1983a 'Defection from new religious movements: A test of some theoretical propositions', in Bromley, D and Richardson, J (Eds), *The Brainwashing/Deprogramming Controversy*, New York: The Edwin Mellen Press: 106-121.

Wright, S 1983b 'A Sociological Study of Defection from Controversial New Religious Movements', Ph.D. dissertation, Ann Arbor, Michigan: University Microfilms International.

Wright, S 1984 'Post involvement attitudes of voluntary defectors from controversial new religious movements', *Journal for the Scientific Study of Religion* 23: 172-82.

Wright, S 1986 'Dyadic intimacy and social control in three cult movements', *Sociological Analysis* 47(2): 137-150.

Wright, S 1987 *Leaving Cults: The Dynamics of Defection*, Washington, DC: Society for the Scientific Study of Religion.

Wright, S 1988   'Leaving new religious movements: Issues, theory, and research', in Bromley, D (Ed), *Falling from the Faith: Causes and Consequences of Religious Apostasy*, Newbury Park, CA: Sage: 143-65.

Wright, S and Piper, E 1986 'Families and cults: Familial factors related to youth leaving and remaining in deviant religious groups', *Journal of Marriage and the Family* 48: 15-25.

9
Assessing RENEW
a Study of a Renewal Movement in a Roman Catholic Diocese in England*

Michael P Hornsby-Smith, John Fulton
and Margaret Norris

The RENEW 'process' commenced in the diocese of Arundel and Brighton, England, in the Autumn of 1988 and is scheduled to conclude in November 1990. RENEW is a diocesan-wide, parish-based pastoral program. In this contribution, we will first outline the origins and development of RENEW, present the levels of analysis at which the research is being undertaken, report some early findings, and finally reflect on some pre-established hypotheses and lines of research for the future. As will be seen, we raise wider issues about processes of 'renewal' in the Roman Catholic Church a quarter of a century after the Second Vatican Council (1962-65), whose specific function was the religious reform of the Church.

RENEW originated in the archdiocese of Newark in the United States in 1976, stimulated apparently by a concern for the failure of Vatican II reforms to re-energize the parish system and the religious lives of laity. Archbishop Gerety set up a nucleus of workers to develop a parish-based renewal program. It was headed by two priests, one of whom was Monsignor Tom Kleissler, who is still prominent in the international organization of RENEW. Since then the program has been promoted in, and taken on by, dioceses throughout North America (Geaney 1987: 63) and, indeed, by over 112 dioceses throughout the world (Kelly 1987: 197). The movement has spread worldwide and clearly merits sociological attention.

The aims of RENEW are varyingly described in the program's literature. One formulation describes them as 'teaching and witnessing to the Word of God', 'developing vibrant faith communities' and 'establishing justice formation and action' (Martin 1980: iv). The means to achieve these goals are the two main features of RENEW, namely its planned themes and its unique organization with 'small groups' at the core. The themes find temporal expression in the five 'seasons', each of which run for six weeks over a period of two and a half years. The consecutive titles of the seasons are 'The Lord's Call', 'Our Response to the Lord's Call', 'Empowerment by the Spirit', 'Discipleship' and 'Evangelization'. Material from the Scriptures

---

*   We are indebted to Ray Lee for helpful comments on an earlier draft of this paper and James R. Kelly for his generous assistance.

and supportive literature expand on the theme, which is meant to be reflected on, prayed about and discussed and which will then hopefully result in some form of religiously motivated action, or 'action-response' as the literature describes it.

The organization of the process is heavily bureaucratized. At the nub of it all are the international RENEW office in Newark, New Jersey, which provides extensive literature and a small team of world-wide travelling experts, and the local diocesan RENEW committee, which may add to or modify the literature for parishes and trains committee and group leaders. At the local parish level, the centre of the concrete process itself, something in the order of twelve committees are set up. The first is the core group of three or four persons, led by the parish RENEW coordinator, who is supposed to be a lay-person. These are the originators of RENEW at parish level, and have the task of setting up the initial organization and recruiting leaders and may come together from time to time to resolve crises or change tack. Then there are the ten central operational committees. Some of these run mainly before a season gets under way and have the purpose of getting parishioners involved and committed to each six week program: the 'sign-up', telephone, prayer network, home visits and publicity committees. Then there are those which run mainly during each season: Sunday liturgy, take home (literature distribution), large group and small group committees, with publicity and home visiting continuing to function. There is then an evaluation committee, assessing the progress of each season, and reporting mainly after the season has ended. A final committee, or 'the Parish Renew Team', is made up of all the committee leaders, who are supposed to meet as often as necessary, providing mutual support while at the same time being a prayer group in the spirit of the program. This leads us to the heart of the program, which is really the small groups of parishioners who have signed on at the beginning of each season to meet regularly for reading and reflection on Scripture and related literature, and for prayer, discussion and faith-sharing. Given the extent of organization such a process entails, it is not surprising to find that, in one commentator's words, 'the national [Newark] RENEW office supplies dioceses with step-by-step program instructions that must rival a modern general's war plans' (Kelly 1987: 197).

Methods and Preliminary Perspectives

Investigation of such a program can be undertaken at three distinct levels of sociological concern. Here we outline them giving some indication of relevant hypotheses and appropriate data. Firstly there is *the global level* where one can focus on the entrepreneurial activity of marketing an American pastoral program throughout the world. One can hypothesize that to some extent RENEW might be a sophisticated economic enterprise marketed by religious entrepreneurs with tangible economic rewards accruing to the archdiocese of Newark. However, though marketing is clearly being done, from what we have gleaned so far from informants, the charge to the diocese of Arundel and Brighton for the use of the RENEW program and materials is said to be only $10,000. In addition, it is well known that the budget of the central RENEW organization in Newark for 1985-6 was $619,913 at a time when the staff numbered thirteen. The monetary sources were quite modest: 'About one-quarter of their funds comes from foundations, about one-third from Paulist Press sales and the rest (just over forty percent) from fees charged for their consulting and training services to dioceses which adopt RENEW' (Kelly c1986: 257).

A further focus at the global level can be cultural. RENEW is American not only in its origins but also in its idiom, forms of expression and assumption of a 'culture of dialogue'. By this phrase we mean that an open, face-to-face style of communication, which is arguably more characteristic of American popular culture than, say, the British, particularly in the field of religious language, is built into the RENEW program. Informants have suggested that RENEW had been 'bought in' as a fairly fixed package, not only by the research diocese, but also by a number of dioceses in Scotland. For financial and resource reasons and its claimed 'proven track record', little modification of the program materials to adapt them to British circumstances was undertaken in the first instance. Its organizational style and recommendations reflect a strong flavour of American managerialism and this has generated some resentment in our research diocese, at least at the parishioner level. Additionally, the extensive organization required suggests a level of human resourcing typical of US parishes, with their larger numbers of full or semi-employed religious and laity. English and Scottish parishes are very much one man concerns, with volunteers being relied upon for almost everything else. The scale of RENEW hardly seems to accord with small parish needs and, in at least one of the two parishes investigated so far, has resulted in considerable stress to parish leaders and a scaling-down operation, seen as both appropriate and inevitable. These facts suggest a certain religious or cultural colonialism. Though clearly unintentional, it does appear that there has been some neglect on matters of cultural and organizational translation.

A second level of inquiry is the *diocesan level* where one is able to examine the initiation of the program and the way it is financed, organized and carried out. In our research diocese, an examination of the process of decision-making in the adoption of the program by the bishop, the majority of the priests in the diocese and lay representatives of parishes, suggested a decision emanating from the top of a hierarchy. It seems that the bishop in our research diocese, unlike a number of other English bishops who also became informed, was persuaded to adopt the program by presentations from the Newark team. Informants have suggested that he saw the program providing at least part of a necessary response to the diocese's institutional decline, as indicated for example by a 25 percent decline in the Sunday Mass attendance figures since 1967 and by a decline in its priest workforce of 22 per cent in the past fifteen years. Only one priest in seven is currently under the age of forty (private communication from two priest informants). Also, within the diocese there have been numerous pleas from lay people for more spiritual formation following on from earlier pastoral programs.

However, a key element in RENEW is supposed to be the free acceptance of the undertaking to carry it out. This element of freedom is stressed in the literature for the First Season of RENEW (the Lord's Call) and at the initial sessions for parish representatives, acting as proxy for the parish as a whole. It is clear that a number of the clergy were sceptical initially and concerned that the program was not 'home-grown'. They found out about the proposal to run RENEW directly from the bishop at a two-hour communal gathering with him, and were asked to indicate their decision at the same meeting on a show of hands. A similar pattern appears to have been followed when the bishop addressed a number of influential laity from around the diocese. Tentatively we suggest that the decision to initiate RENEW was pre-empted by the bishop and that agreement to participate by nearly all the parishes in the diocese was only obtained *post facto* and hardly on the basis of informed consent. Priests and key laity were incorporated into the planning of the program long before they had been shown details of what it entailed.

A second hypothesis at the diocesan level of inquiry is that diocesan leaders may have gone ahead with RENEW without adequate specification of resource implications at either diocesan or parish level. In a sense, there is an in-built protection against genuine resource appraisal in RENEW, as it is supposed to mushroom and draw in people previously inactive in the Church. However, we suggest that a proper evaluation of the RENEW program would take into account alternative uses of monetary resources and incorporate extensive consultations within the diocese. We suspect that this has not been done.

A third level of sociological inquiry into RENEW is *the parish level*. Here one can consider the impact of the RENEW program in terms of the changes brought about in priest-parishioner relationships, the levels and kinds of interaction between parishioners themselves, in personal religious consciousness and in the amount and types of religious activity. To approach such issues, it is necessary to relate the proclaimed aims of RENEW to empirical social and religious outcomes. The next section presents some preliminary findings from the research at parish level after the first two 'seasons' in the autumn of 1988 and the spring of 1989.

The research which has so far been undertaken includes all three levels presented above, though with a particular focus on the local or parish level. The techniques adopted in the research include content analysis of documentary materials and other background sources relating to the RENEW program and the claims of its sponsors. Taped focused interviews with key informants at the international, diocesan and parish levels have been obtained. In two parishes, case studies have been undertaken involving both participant and non-participant observation by all members of the research team. Finally, participation in the evaluation process required in each parish has been pursued, in particular by means of questionnaire surveys of parishioners, small group members and leaders. In sum, a variety of both qualitative and quantitative research methods have been employed. In future work we hope to extend the range of parishes studied comparatively. We also plan to intensify our investigations of those who have dropped out of small groups in order to replicate some of the work of Maureen Gallagher with 'dropouts' and 'persisters' in the United States (Kelly c1986: 110-25). Finally, we intend to explore further, for example in focused interviews, the interpretations held by that large minority of parishioners who have not participated in the RENEW process, at least some of whom have been alienated by what they see as an intrusion into the parish life they have come to expect.

The Parish Evaluation Process: Some Preliminary Findings

A feature of the RENEW program is its evaluation procedures at the end of each season. This presents the participant-researcher with an unusually favourable climate within the Catholic parishes which are normally suspicious and hostile towards what are often regarded as alien social scientific enquiries. Each parish is required to evaluate all its activities and processes during each season. According to the instructions in the RENEW Information Packet, the Evaluation Committee in each parish is not to be concerned with '...*evaluation at the end of an effort or project* to determine whether it did what it was supposed to do, was worth the cost, should have been done better, or perhaps should not have been undertaken at all,' but with *developmental evaluation* which is '...*conducted while an effort is in progress*, to make sure that it is on the right track and is being well executed, in order to correct the situation while the project is still in progress' (Martin 1980: 77 - italics added). In a later paper, we will return to the question of this interpretation of developmental evaluation. However, we must say briefly that the way this is being carried out in RENEW almost certainly fails to meet the accepted canons for professional evaluation. Moreover, a key informant regarded the evaluation process not so much as any developmental enquiry but as a heaven-sent opportunity to find out something about what is going on in the 112 parishes in the diocese and especially indicators of priest-lay relationships and of independent lay participation.

Whatever the motivation for collecting this information, data are now available which show that the proportion of Mass attenders who had participated in small groups during Season One of RENEW varied from 5 to 60 per cent and there were also big differences between parishes in the extent to which they had attempted some form of 'outreach' work, as indicated by the number of home visits made. In 1988, in the research diocese the reported Mass attendance figures, including children, were 52,436. The diocesan RENEW office reports that at the end of Season One, in November 1988, 13,956 people (in 70 of the 112 parishes) 'made a prayer commitment', 12,369 participated in the small groups and 1,274 people 'have become involved' as a result of the work of the Home Visiting and/or Telephone groups. It is also reported that 'Prayerfulness, a growing sense of community and a new-found facility in turning to the Scriptures as a source for personal and group prayer and faith-sharing - these have been the most commonly experienced fruits of RENEW in Season One' (Arundel and Brighton 1989a).

Part of our own research has been opportunistic and we have exploited the fact that two of us have been members of the Evaluation Committee in a relatively progressive parish about thirty miles from London. Detailed accounts of the post-Vatican orientation of this parish have been given by the former parish priest (O'Sullivan 1979) and in a recent analysis of *The Changing Parish* (Hornsby-Smith 1989). The Mass attendance in this parish in 1987 was 513 according to Arundel and Brighton (1989b). But it is likely that this has not grown concomitantly with the population expansion resulting from recently completed housing estates within the parish boundaries.

In this parish, key instruments in the evaluation process at the end of Season One in November 1988 and Season Two in April 1989 were two self-completion questionnaires, one delivered to all Mass attenders (16 years and over) during Mass and the other to all members of the small groups. Some demographic data were also collected, up to the limit of what was judged to be tolerable, and this facilitated a small amount of analysis of the returns. By repeating our surveys over the five seasons of RENEW it is hoped to explore further variations by age, gender, occupational status and spacial location within the parish, and also between small group 'dropouts' and continuing members or 'persisters'.

199 people signed up in the parish for the small group meetings in Season One and 211 in Season Two. This was two-fifths of the total Mass attenders or an estimated three-fifths of the adult attenders. 18 of the 23 group leaders and 144 small group members completed evaluation questionnaires at the end of Season One and 19 of the 21 group leaders and 169 small group members at the end of Season Two. The results indicated that 82 per cent of those who had signed up attended at least one meeting and were then likely to persevere in Season One. In Season Two this proportion increased to around 96 per cent. On average, members attended five of the six meetings which usually lasted about two hours. Numbers attending the groups in the first season varied considerably, from 3 to 12. As a result of policy decisions, group sizes in Season Two were evened up to 9 to 13. Groups, which were constructed mainly on the basis of geographical location and preferred meeting time, varied considerably in their composition. Most participants were married and female. Overall three times as many women as men took part in the

group work and there was a noticeable absence of teenagers and people in their twenties in Season One. In Season Two there were two groups for teenagers. Some groups meeting during the day were all-female. Some were homogeneous in terms of age or occupation, while others were more representative of the range in the parish. About one-fifth to one-quarter of the members in groups lived outside the geographical boundaries of the parish.

Some variations in the styles of group work were reflected in the open-ended comments of members. Not all groups followed the recommended RENEW format closely and some groups were led as discussion groups rather than faith-sharing groups. In Season One, one member in ten observed that the leaders manifestly had no training and no intuitive skills in controlling the contributions of members, particularly in extempore prayer and the more charismatic aspects of group work. Of those people who did participate in prayer periods, as many as one in five felt very uncomfortable. This may reflect the fact that even in this relatively progressive parish, with its long tradition of house-groups, as many as two-fifths of the RENEW group members in Season One had not attended a group previously. Many of the 'newcomers' found much of the discussion, prayer and faith-sharing intimidating, given the ritualised passivity of many Catholics. But experienced group members often reflected a weary sense of *déjà vu* more than two decades after the end of the Second Vatican Council. In Season Two, many of these criticisms were reduced, but many members wanted more attention paid to spiritual growth, discussion and prayer.

Our second major source of data came from the 248 questionnaires completed by adult attenders during Mass on the last Sunday of Season One and the 245 questionnaires completed during Mass three weeks after Season Two. Parishioners were led through the questionnaire by the parish priest and the whole exercise lasted between five and ten minutes. The response rate was just under one half of all Mass attenders and an estimated 70 per cent of adult attenders. Allowing for a few visitors and other people, the scale of the non-response might be regarded as one measure of resistance to what some considered to be an intrusion of 'profane' social science into the 'sacred' time of the Mass.

The results complemented those from the small group survey and indicated that two-thirds of parishioners claimed to have prayed more during Season One and that a similar proportion had read the specially selected daily Scripture reflections in a booklet distributed free to all parishioners before the commencement of Season One. Both proportions appear to have increased slightly in Season Two. In both seasons half had read these daily or most days, the rest sometimes.

Some lack of clarity in the specification of the goals of RENEW appeared in the responses at the end of Season One. More than one quarter of parishioners were unable to describe the goals at all. About one-third described 'community' as an aim, generally in a fairly local form referring to family, neighbourhood, friendships, parishioners, or the relationship between the parish and the diocese. Some of these included the wider or global community and so probably incorporated a dimension of social justice. Two-thirds gave renewal of spiritual life or faith as an aim, some through reading the Word of God. About 6 per cent of the respondents mentioned evangelism either with reference to non-Catholics or to the 'lapsed'.

Overall more than half the respondents thought that RENEW had made some difference to their lives at the end of both Seasons One and Two. Of those who commented, about three-quarters were in favour of RENEW by the end of Season One, though some only mildly, and the rest were opposed. One person in eight thought that community spirit had been promoted in some way while one in ten thought they had benefited by personal development of some kind. Women over 35 were more likely to have participated than men or the young of either sex, though people's view of RENEW was much the same, regardless of age or sex. At the end of Season Two around 83 per cent of the parishioner respondents reported themselves very or fairly satisfied with RENEW.

At the end of Season One, nine aspects of small group activity were identified from members' comments. In the evaluation of Season Two, members of the partially reconstructed groups were invited to select from these the two they considered most important and the two they considered least important. The results, summarised in Table 1, indicate that the elements of faith-sharing, discussion, making new friends and praying more were selected most strongly. A growing awareness of the worldwide

Table 1: Two Most Important and Two Least Important Aspects of Small Groups
(Small Group Members' Questionnaire, Season Two) (N=162)

Aspect	Most Imp	Least Imp	Net Imp.
Prayed more or better	43	10	+33
More self-aware, confident, personal development	28	49	-21
More awareness of worldwide community	10	64	-54
Better communication with family, friends	15	17	-2
Stimulated discussion	45	17	+28
Made new friends	54	16	+38
More interest in scripture	33	25	+8
Stimulated to take part in parish, or local community	6	41	-35
More open sharing feelings about faith with others	80	18	+62

community, stimulation to become more involved in the parish and personal development were all regarded as of little importance. However, when invited to indicate to which aspects members would prefer to pay more attention in Season Three, the responses were more evenly spread (Table 2). One-third wanted to see more emphasis on personal or group spiritual growth and over one-quarter a greater emphasis on prayer. For one-quarter more emphasis on discussion was suggested. About one member in seven wanted to see a greater stress on action in each of three categories: the wider community, the home and the parish.

Development of Perspectives

In 1985 a Fordham University Professor of Sociology, James Kelly, evaluated the RENEW program for the Lilly Endowment. He concluded that the results were 'modest' (c1986: 248) and that 'RENEW "works", but not quite as dramatically as its sponsors claimed' (Kelly 1987: 197-8). He commented on the avoidance of controversial issues with 'many men and women seek(ing) mostly to deepen their attachment to the core elements of the average Christian life: the Scriptures, the Mass, prayer, uncomplicated fellowship and support' but expressed 'some unease about RENEW's avoidance of doctrinal disputes'. He suggested fears of 'an unhealthy parish pietism' might have been exaggerated and that while 'RENEW does not push too hard... the distinction between charity and justice... receives more attention than the materials themselves might suggest'. This was reflected in an increase in the number of parishes with Social Concern Committees. The process of RENEW involves large numbers of lay leaders, especially women, essential as the Church faces the decline in the number of priests and encourages small group discussion on the controversial issues raised by the American bishops in their pastoral letters on peace and on economic justice. In sum, Kelly concludes that RENEW sought 'to provoke piety not passion' (1987: 197-9).

The research undertaken by Kelly in the USA is the first attempt at an overall sociological interpretation of RENEW. On the basis of his work he suggested that

Table 2: Preferred Greater Emphasis for Season Three
(Small Group Members' Questionnaire: Season Two) (All mentions; N=162)

Prayer	41
Personal and group spiritual growth	56
Scripture reading	21
Discussion	44
Action, related to weekly themes, in the home	23
Action, related to weekly themes, in the parish	22
Action, related to weekly themes, in the wider community	26

RENEW... is a contemporary example of a pietistic solution to the problems of anomie. Like all such movements, it seeks to anchor religious identity in religious affections which do not depend on creedal clarity and intellectualized faith. It is an example of a religious revitalization movement which occurs during times of transition.... RENEW illustrates the possibility of religious revivals that affirm institutional allegiance even without offering convincing solutions to institutional dilemmas... so that the primary religious functions for the average believer can be affirmed and exercised, namely, the rousing of religious affections around the central faith symbols. RENEW represents a Catholic version of pietism (c1986: 261, 263).

Kelly has suggested that RENEW can be regarded as a revitalisation movement. The application of this term to institutionalised religion in a modern institutionally plural society is perhaps a little stretched. According to its originator Wallace (1956), such movements are typical of total cultural upheaval and decay in societies, and are attempts to regenerate the group with a more satisfying culture. Examples would be the Mau-Mau in Kenya, Cargo Cults and the American Indian ghost dance, all responses to white, Western imperialism. Clearly there are dimensions of such movements present in what are perhaps better and simply called *renewal movements*, of which there is a long history within the Christian Churches. It is clear also that a sociological understanding of the RENEW program has to be seen against this historical development, and part of the present research program is devoted to this task.

A feature of revitalization movements which might be shared by renewal movements is the high degree of stress and disillusionment which individuals experience within the old cultural frame of reference. From this viewpoint RENEW might be seen as a response to the status-anxiety of clergy, or their perception of institutional decline, or as a response to what they might see as a disappointing failure to evangelise on the part of a cosy, complacent, and indeed domesticated post-Vatican Church. There can be little doubt also that dissatisfaction among committed laity is widespread, either with the changes which have occurred within the Church since the 1960s (for example, the replacement of the Tridentine ritual and of individualized, devotional forms of prayer) or with the failure to implement so many of the reforms the Second Vatican Council promised (neglect of the massive problems of the contemporary world, such as hunger and war).

There are also indications within the RENEW program of a search to bring together the two opposing wings of discontent on the basis of a pietistic and parish-centred solution. There are signs in our research data that such concerns take priority over a wider social awareness. Whatever the goals of the RENEW promoters, Catholics in the research parish were primarily socially constructing a revitalised personal piety and devotionalism and also promoting and welcoming the development of more friendships and community-building occasions in the parish. In general, a greater concern with scripture was not strongly emphasised. Nor was a concern with 'action-response' - the application of their religious faith in their everyday lives, not only in their homes and in the parish but also in the wider world - at all prominent. But more detailed comparative data is necessary to confirm these findings. It will also be necessary to undertake further analysis to see if such results are more a function of the way RENEW is used rather than inherent in its goals and organizational structure.

Two hypotheses which suggest that the structure itself might be determinant in this way were made early on in our research, and before the commencement of Season One in the autumn of 1988, and relate to processes apparent in the preparation of the program at diocesan and parish level.

Firstly, we suggested that, at the parish level, the goals of the RENEW process were unclear and that no adequate specification of them was forthcoming from the team responsible for initiating RENEW in the diocese. Ambiguity in the specification of the goals of the program has implications for the evaluation process built into the RENEW program. Measurements of virtually any aspect of parochial life could be seen *ex post facto* as evidence of success. It may be objected that the 'aims' of RENEW are listed in the literature and some presentation of them was made to parish groups on their first training session with the diocesan leaders. However, aims such as 'the development of vibrant faith communities' are not very precise. In addition, in the resource materials different aims are listed in different places. It is also clear from claims about the success of RENEW in the local diocesan newsletter that there has been as yet no attempt to disentangle data on RENEW-related action from data about other events, prayer-groups and activities. Some of these would have been going on anyway even without the RENEW program.

Secondly, it was suggested that a process of goal-displacement appeared to be taking place at both diocesan and parish level and that an instrumental value had replaced a terminal value (Merton 1957), that is that a bureaucratic obsession with *means* had replaced a concern for the original goals of the RENEW organisation. Merton terms this the 'ritualist' form of deviance. Whether this is intrinsic to the RENEW package or a result of imposing the scale of large American parishes on to small English ones (assuming for the moment that the two issues are distinct), there does seem to be a great deal of effort being put into specifying *means* to be adopted in the parishes: the setting-up of core groups, selection of leaders, program for Sign-Up Sunday for small groups, arrangements for door-step calling on known but dormant Catholics, and so on. As already reported, the lack of human resources to complete and maintain such an extensive organization has resulted in a considerable scaling down of the RENEW operation in one of our research parishes. At the wider level, the limited materials which were available in advance of Season One all stressed the procedures required in each parish: the task of the core leadership group, the dozen or so committees which needed to be formed if RENEW was to be successful, the timing and sequencing of the various events from Sign-Up Sunday, and so on. Surprisingly little specification of the purposes of all this activity was available in advance. From what we have gleaned from several sources around the diocese, it appears that Catholics were simply urged to participate in the RENEW process and considerable moral pressure was put on those who were sceptical, especially in those parishes which already had small group programs which had been developed over many years. However, the extent to which participation in RENEW was regarded as an indication of loyalty and commitment is a matter for further empirical enquiry.

The pressure in such situations is to take quantity as a sign of quality. It may be that Catholics are simply being invited to participate in more parish activities. Indeed, one of the claims made for RENEW is that the proportion of active parishioners is substantially increased. Kelly suggests that these are really quite modest with 'small group participation of between 6 and 10 per cent' (c1986: 148).

This, however, begs a number of questions. First of all it can be argued that the proportion of Catholics, whether nominal or Mass attending, who are involved in the activities of the institutional Church (as stewards, readers, special ministers, members of parish organisations, and so on) is not the only relevant indicator of the religious commitment and vitality of the parish. Thus it has been argued (Hornsby-Smith 1989) that there are signs in the post-Vatican Church that the greater participation of lay people has led to an increased concern with 'churchy' affairs in a 'greedy' institution (Coser 1974) rather than, for example, with the educational task of 'forming' lay people to work for the transformation of social structures in ways which accord better with the imperatives of social justice.

A major reservation about the RENEW process, then, is that it might greedily consume all the discretionary time and energy of active parishioners and so further reduce the time and energy available to them for their roles as 'lay apostles' in secular institutions such as professional associations, trade unions, local government and pressure groups. It has yet to be seen if the work of the justice and peace groups in the parishes is likely to suffer if attention is focused on more 'spiritual' or devotional concerns. One member of the diocesan RENEW team has observed that in Newark it had taken several years to move 'from effects to causes'. However, whether or not there was a delayed reaction in Newark, the RENEW process appears to have encouraged in Newark some response to social problems, for example in the form of the provision of soup kitchens. But it is not clear whether attention has been further focused sufficiently on identifying the social causes of these problems and on the religious need to be more politically active in seeking appropriate solutions.

Conclusion

Financial questions, the pre-empting of choice in the initiation of the program, the pietistic orientation of the program at least in the early seasons, and the problems of goals and goal-displacement, do suggest the relevance of long-standing questions concerned with centralised, hierarchical social control in the development of renewal movements within Roman Catholicism. Some movements, for example many of the early religious orders of monks and friars, originated outside the established hierarchical order of bishops and priests. Such renewal movements always and eventually came under clerical control which became increasingly centralised after the Council of Trent (1545-63). In recent times, the charismatic renewal movement received the blessing of the Church, but a degree of centralized control went with it. So far, this has not been the case for the base communities which still escape complete hierarchical domestication. RENEW however has been promoted from the top of regional Church organization. Are we up against the contradiction of seeking to make spontaneous that which is intrinsically planned and programmed? Is any spark of vitality or renewal which goes beyond the pietistic to be expected of this particular program and process? A focal concern of our investigation is the extent to which clerical control is strictly maintained over the RENEW process: its materials and the manner of their adaptation to local circumstances, the sequencing of the program, and the scope for lay initiatives in the consideration of emergent issues and in the choice of action alternatives arising out of the process. We aim to address the question of whether RENEW is a sophisticated device for increasing the proportion of active members in the internal institutional concerns of the Church, or whether it is intended to raise the awareness of Catholics to the relationship between the Christian gospel and the wider world. We also aim to consider whether it approximates more closely to the devotional concerns of the charismatic movement or to the socio-political concerns of the base communities. We wish to discern whether its aims are primarily 'personal' or 'community' development and whether it will increase the level of lay involvement in the 'greedy' parish and its work of localised 'social concern' at the expense of a sharpening of a concern for social justice in the wider society.

Issues of social control and creativity are difficult to handle in a scientific way. We hope to further understanding in this area by applying also the analysis of qualitative 'soft' data developed by Margaret Norris for the study of community development (1977, 1981). On the basis of this work, we concur in distinguishing four RENEWAL styles as a framework to analyse directive and non-directive organizational characteristics, and traditional and progressive religious concerns. Data derived from the RENEW literature and from conversations and interviews are being analyzed using this frame.

In sum, our early findings on RENEW suggest that by the end of Season Two, community-building and personal spirituality goals were seen by participants as more important than missionary or social action goals. The expansion of justice and peace work in the diocese and the growth of a socio-religious consciousness beyond the spiritual and physical limits of parish and diocese may yet emerge in the later seasons. If they do, Kelly's view of RENEW as predominantly pietistic would be questioned, at least for our research diocese, and RENEW would be seen as capable also of other things in the field of religious consciousness and action.

Bibliography

Coser, L A 1974 *Greedy Institutions: Patterns of Undivided Commitment*, New York: Free Press; London: Collier-Macmillan.

Arundel and Brighton, 1989a 'Summary of Parish Evaluations - Season One', Arundel: Diocesan RENEW Office.

Arundel and Brighton, 1989b *Diocesan Directory*, Arundel: Diocese of Arundel and Brighton.

Geaney, D J 1987 *Quest for Community: Tomorrow's Parish Today*, Notre Dame, Indiana: Ave Maria Press.

Hornsby-Smith, M P 1989 *The Changing Parish: A Study of Parishes, Priests and Parishioners After Vatican II*, London: Routledge.

Kelly, J R c1986 *A Study of the 'RENEW' Program and some of its impacts: Report to the Lilly Endowment Inc.*, New York: Fordham University.

Kelly, J R 1987 'Does the RENEW Program Renew?', *America*, 156/9 (7 March): 197-9.

Martin C 1980 *Leadership Book (Renew)*, Newark: Paulist Press.

Merton, R K 1957 *Social Theory and Social Structure*, New York: Free Press.

Norris, M 1977 'A Formula for Identifying Styles of Community Work', *Community Development Journal*, 12: 22-9.

Norris, M 1981 'Problems in the Analysis of Soft Data and Some Suggested Solutions', *Sociology* 15: 337-51.

O'Sullivan, B 1979 *Parish Alive*, London: Sheed and Ward.

Wallace, A F C 1956 'Revitalization Movements', *American Anthropology* 58: 264-81.

10
Cooperation and Conflict Between Veteran and Immigrant Jews in Swansea 1895-1915^{**}

Leonard Mars

In the past most studies about British Jews have focused on London (Gartner 1986). But recently there has been a switch to provincial towns and cities (Alderman 1972, 1979, Kokosalakis 1982, Henriques 1988, Williams 1976, Josephs 1980, 1984, Collins 1987, Gartner 1981). This chapter reflects that trend and examines Swansea's Jewish community from 1895 to 1915 during which period a group of immigrants from Eastern Europe broke away from the Swansea Hebrew Congregation (hereafter SHC), to form their own synagogue, the *Bes Ha Midrash* (hereafter BHM). 1895 is chosen because a key source, the Minutes Book of the SHC, and other documents survive from that date.

This chapter examines relations between the established, anglicised members of Swansea's community and their immigrant co-religionists. Secession from the SHC was potentially bitter and there was initial opposition not only from leaders of the SHC but also the Chief Rabbi of Great Britain and the British Empire, Dr Herman Adler. However, hostility between the 'English shul' and the BHM was tempered by their common interests as Jews: sharing the same cemetery; concern for Eastern European Jewry; efforts to challenge the passing of the Aliens Act of 1905 directed against the influx of Eastern European Jews; responses to the Zionist movement founded in 1897; and the taking of services by ministers of the SHC in the BHM. Indeed, several people were affiliated to both congregations.

From 1881 Eastern European Jewish immigration into Britain increased (Gartner 1973), especially after the assassination of Tsar Alexander II and of subsequent legislation against Jews. Most Jews migrated to the USA, but approximately 120,000 entered Britain between 1881-1914. The majority settled in the East End of London but many moved into Manchester, Leeds, Glasgow and other cities and towns, among them Swansea.

What sort of Jewish community were the immigrants entering? A brief history of the congregation and its constitution clarifies this question.

---

^{**}This paper is based on a research project on Swansea's Jewish Community funded in part by the Memorial Foundation for Jewish Culture, New York, and on an earlier grant from the Manpower Services Commission (MSC) to the Swansea Hebrew Congregation. I am grateful to Dr Saunders and to Dr Ursula Henriques for their collaboration on the MSC project, to the Trainee archivists, Helen Redmond-Cooper and Kevin Murphy and to Mrs C Cook for assistance with the manuscript.

As an organisation, Swansea's Jewish community dates from 1768 when David Michael leased a plot of land from the municipality for use as a cemetery (Saunders 1980). The consecration of ground for burial before construction of a synagogue is common among Jews. Several buildings served as synagogues until 1859 when the Chief Rabbi's son, Herman Adler, opened Goat Street Synagogue.

The SHC was highly stratified both economically and socially and its structure was embodied in its Rules (SHCa 1892) which stipulated an elaborate ranking of seat-holding. For men seats were ranked in six categories, the most expensive closest to the Ark of the Law that houses the sacred scrolls:

> All seats in the Synagogue shall be arranged and classed in the following order: Class A, 3s 6d per week; Class B, 3s per week; Class C, 2s 6d per week; Class D, 2s per week; Class E, 1s 6d per week; Class F, 1s per week.'... 'Ladies seats in gallery: Class A, 1s per week; Class B, 6d per week.' (SHCa 1892: Rule 21 [s = shilling; d = pence].

Those who paid for seats were entitled to buy Kosher meat and enjoy a guaranteed seat in the synagogue, but payment for a seat did not qualify a person for the status of seatholder, which status was clearly defined in rule 23a:

> A seatholder shall be a person who for 13 consecutive weeks pays a sum of not less than eighteen pence weekly (exclusive of any seat in the ladies' gallery), and until that period has elapsed shall not be entitled to any privileges of the congregation, except that of kosher meat and a seat in the Synagogue. If he wishes to obtain all the privileges he must pay 13 weeks' subscriptions in advance, then apply in writing, and must be proposed, seconded, and balloted for; if elected, he shall be entitled to vote and attend meetings as a privileged member (SHCa 1892).

The same rule indicates how a seatholder could make the transition to 'privileged member' - the mere act of paying at least 18 pence per week was insufficient since a seatholder's application could be rejected by the privileged members, a situation that had occurred (e.g. the case of Mr T Shepherd SHCa 1904: 16 May).

In summary there were three categories of membership:

(a) subscribers, (b) seatholders, and (c) privileged members.

Subscribers - the lowest category - were women, those paying one shilling or less per week and non-residents of Swansea who occasionally visited the Synagogue. Those who paid for a seat became affiliated to the SHC and had certain rights: to burial in the Jewish cemetery, to buy kosher meat at the licensed butcher, to use the *mikvah* or ritual bath, to send children free to the Hebrew and Religion classes, to a Jewish marriage ceremony, and to the services of the *mohel* in circumcising sons. Several of these involved extra expenses, offerings and fees for the officiating minister, fees for the *ketubah* or marriage contract, costs to hire the *chupah* or wedding canopy, and fees for digging a grave. Non-members might receive these services, but at greater cost, including fees for *mohel* and tombstone and requiring a considerable donation to synagogue funds.

Privileged members constituted an elite of seatholders but their own ranks were also stratified. Difficult as it was to make the transition from seatholder to privileged member, so too to progress from privileged member to Committee Man and thence to Treasurer or President. Rule 23 stated:

A member to be eligible for Committee Man must have paid not less than 2s weekly for 52 consecutive weeks, exclusive of the ladies' gallery seat (if any).

To become President or Treasurer rule 23b stipulated:

Members eligible for the office of President or Treasurer, must be resident in Swansea and have subscribed in Class A, B or C (exclusive of the ladies' gallery seat, if any), to the funds of the congregation for a period of not less than two consecutive years.

To hold office or to administer the Congregation, a member had to contribute at least £5 4s 0d. per annum. The balance sheet for 1899-1900 reveals that a tiny group of members controlled an ever-increasing number of people. Of the 95 members in 1899-1900 27 were eligible for the Committee, and only 24 for the post of President or Treasurer.

The privileges of privileged members were those of political power which were closely linked to the classification of seats. The lowest category of privileged members, E seatholders, who had paid 1s 6d a week for at least 13 weeks could vote at General Meetings. The D seatholders who had paid 2s per week for at least 52 weeks could serve on the Committee of Management, an Executive of seven members elected at the AGM. Seatholders in classes C to A who had paid at least 2s 6d per week for two consecutive years could become office-holders, i.e. Wardens, namely Treasurer and President (who had to have served as Treasurer) and Auditors.

The linking of political privileges to seat rents ensured that synagogue government was limited to an oligarchy which restricted admission to its ranks. These men differed in background, religiosity, social philosophy and social class from their Eastern European co-religionists who were settling in South Wales. They were all established and respectable (two, Michael Jacobs and Hyam Goldberg, had become JPs).

The synagogue, as noted, provided diverse services to its members and assisted the poor including the welfare of widows and orphans. All these services cost money, mainly spent on the salaries of the minister, the reader, the beadle and teaching assistants. 81% of the income from subscriptions to SHC was spent on wages and salaries in 1899-1900.

The arrival of numerous immigrants strained the finances, organisation and management of the SHC and caused conflict between the newcomers and the established members. The immigrant Jew in Swansea faced a communal institution, the synagogue, which regulated much of his daily life over which he had no control because he was disenfranchised, though he contributed 1s if married and 6d if single. It was taxation without representation.

The first indication in the Minutes Book of a faction within the SHC is found in 1895 when a series of letters were exchanged between Mr Hyam Goldberg, Mr S Lyons, President of the SHC, and Dr Adler, the Chief Rabbi. Dr Adler, writing to Mr Goldberg, remarked that he had received several letters from 'poor foreign workmen in your congregation' (SHCa 1895: letters of 9 Dec) complaining that since they could not afford the congregation's dues they had been refused kosher meat, a monopoly of the SHC since it employed the only *shochet*, ritual slaughterer, licensed by the Chief Rabbi, in town. In protest the immigrants had sworn an oath not to eat the SHC's meat and had requested their own *shochet* from the Chief Rabbi.

Dr Adler regretted the situation which he perceived as schism but he also recognised the coercive force of the collective oath and proposed that a *shochet* from another congregation serve the immigrants. Realistically, he pointed out that if he failed to provide a *shochet* the oath-takers could easily recruit: 'one of a great number of poor, starving *shochetim* who have escaped from Russia and are in this country'.

Mr Goldberg passed the Chief Rabbi's letter to the President, who replied on the same day explaining the SHC had resolved that the congregation's married men had to pay a minimum of 1s per week if they wanted the privileges of membership. He pointed out that the protestors only paid 6d per week yet enjoyed all privileges. Consequently, the general body had decided that men who refused to pay the 1s should be charged a meat tax of one penny per week though the decision had not been implemented. The President alleged that the plaintiffs were not so destitute:

> Your experience of this class is I am sure greater than mine and as you are aware they all plead poverty, they certainly cannot be in the low circumstances they would make you believe when I tell you that some of them pay from 1s to 2s 6d per week for Hebrew education and will not avail themselves of the Hebrew school (which is free) provided by the congregation.

Justifying the SHC's position, the President sent the Chief Rabbi the balance sheet of the congregation which was running in deficit; he urged Dr Adler to refuse the plaintiffs a *shochet* since that would reduce the income of the SHC, deprive the children of a teacher (since he combined the posts of *shochet* and teacher), and undermine the authority of the officers of SHC. He observed that despite the oath some of the plaintiffs still purchased meat from the SHC.

The situation escalated when Mr Rutter arrived in London to seek a *shochet* from the Chief Rabbi. Dr Adler informed Mr Lyons of this development on December 17 and outlined his dilemma (SHCa 1895: letters). He remarked that Mr Rutter, representing the 'dissidents', as the Chief Rabbi styled them, would appear before the rabbinical court (*beth din*), to request a *shochet* and that if he was refused 'I am certain they will obtain one without my permission.' He bade Mr Lyons 'suggest a means of reconciliation' before Mr Rutter's petition.

The following day Mr Lyons replied to the Chief Rabbi and reproached Mr Rutter's behaviour as a member of the SHC; he beseeched Dr Adler to deny Rutter a *shochet* and observed: 'If they are as poor as they would make you believe, how are they going to pay the necessary expenses of a congregation of their own which I am sure will cost them individually much more than 1/- per week.'

The correspondence continued, mainly about the character of Mr Rutter, who had written to Dr Adler stating that the dispute had been resolved and that the SHC no longer opposed the recruitment by the 'foreign members' of a teacher/*shochet*. The Chief Rabbi may have doubted the veracity of Mr Rutter's letter since he sent a copy to Mr Lyons and requested confirmation of its accuracy. In reply the President rejected Rutter's claims and informed Dr Adler that 'with the exception of three persons the whole of the "opposition" is prepared to make peace'; he concluded optimistically that 'things will right themselves at an early date'. This reply, together with information from Mr Hyam Goldberg about prospects of reconciliation with the dissidents convinced the Chief Rabbi to deny Mr Rutter his *shochet*.

What does this correspondence signify about relations between the leaders of the 'English synagogue' and their 'foreign members' and about the Chief Rabbi's role in a rapidly changing Anglo-Jewish community?

To answer these questions we should recognise that Swansea's case reflected the national scene where East European Jews encountered local Jewish elites, themselves either immigrants or their children of an earlier period (see Gartner 1961, Henriques 1988, Shaftesbury 1970, Sharot 1976). These earlier immigrants, mainly of German origin, had acculturated to English middle class values and had become part of the Victorian British bourgeoisie (*ibid.* and also Joseph 1980, 1984, Kokosolakis 1982, Williams 1976).

The arrival of impoverished, Eastern European, Yiddish-speaking Jews fleeing from multiple forms of oppression, economic, political and religious, presented both a challenge and a problem to local and national Jewish leaders. As fellow Jews they were due assistance but this was conditional on their affiliation to the established congregations led by privileged members - a condition challenged by the newcomers.

Dr Herman Adler, born in 1839 in Hanover, came to Britain in 1842 when his father Dr Nathan Adler was appointed Chief Rabbi. He held a post that did not exist in Eastern Europe where rabbis were ranked by their piety and scholarship rather than by formal office. Consequently, the Eastern European Jews, though prepared to approach and negotiate with him, did not accept the legitimacy of his position unlike the lay leaders of provincial and metropolitan Jewry. Aware of his vulnerability, the Chief Rabbi sought to reconcile the veteran congregants and the new immigrants.

Dr Adler's initial letter was not to the President of the SHC but to one of the most powerful men in the community, Mr Hyam Goldberg, who forwarded it to the President. Mr Hyam Goldberg's father, Simon Goldberg, was on the committee of the SHC in 1859 when Herman Adler, representing his own father, performed his first public duty in consecrating the new synagogue. The already long relationship between Dr Adler and Mr Goldberg was to persist into the early years of the 20th century especially during Mr Goldberg's presidency (1902-4). It was Mr Goldberg's continued contact with Dr Adler that persuaded him to reject the appointment of a *shochet*.

The Chief Rabbi enjoyed frequent and regular contact (SHCa 1895-1909, c1902-4) with Swansea's leaders who, like him, were the anglicised, Victorian, Jewish gentlemen who had prospered in British society. Both Hyam Goldberg, a prosperous coal exporter and ship's broker, a member of the Conservative Party and Justice of the Peace, and Herman Adler were the sons of German Jewish immigrants who identified strongly with Britain and the ideas of progress and self-improvement. The Chief Rabbi's reference to 'poor, foreign workmen in your congregation' indicates the perception of his generation's place in British society and also that of the newcomers. The phrase is based on a set of words that combines differentiation with solidarity - thus 'poor' is contrasted with rich, 'foreign' with English (rather than British) and 'workmen' with gentlemen. However, these polar opposites are linked together in a single congregation of Jews led by the rich, English gentlemen who represented the Chief Rabbi.

The words 'in your congregation' show the hold of the élite over ordinary congregants. In the case of the Goldbergs this idea of the congregation as a personal possession is enshrined in the 1892 Book of Rules where Mr Simon Goldberg became entitled 'during his lifetime to retain possession of the Congregation's 'trust deeds, documents and securities'. (Rule 10a). In addition, Mr Goldberg was to 'officiate as *Batifila* [prayer leader] and *Batekea* (shofar blower), on every occasion as long as he thinks fit, and when he decides to discontinue same, no other private member be allowed to act as *Batifila* or *Batekea*.' (Rule 23)

In appealing to the Chief Rabbi, the immigrants acknowledged his authority over the Congregation's élite and over themselves as subscribers to the SHC. However, both parties recognised their fragile relationship and the potential for rupture. Hence the Chief Rabbi's initial preparedness to grant a *shochet* since the immigrants could easily acquire one outside of his jurisdiction. The immigrants invoked his support as lowly members of the congregation but both parties were aware that they could sever ties, which Dr Adler sought to avoid by reference to 'reconciliation' and in his plea to the President: 'I hope you and your colleagues will be successful in preventing a split which I would deplore as much as you.' (SHCa 1885: 19 Dec)

The Chief Rabbi had reason to maintain the congregation's unity since a breakaway group composed of immigrants, but led by some members of the SHC, e.g. Mr Rutter, might reject his authority. Indeed Swansea's problem was familiar since in 1887 immigrant synagogues in East London had formed a Federation of Minor Synagogues presided over by Samuel Montagu, MP, later Lord Swaythling, a grouping that rivalled the Chief Rabbi's organisation, the United Synagogue Movement ('minor' was a euphemism for *chevra* [immigrant synagogue] Shaftesbury 1970: 104).

The President also wished to retain the immigrants within his congregation since their secession would have repercussions for the SHC; economically , recognition of a rival *shochet* would reduce its income from meat sales; politically weaken the SHC and its leadership by creating a separate Jewish organisation; reduce the size of the SHC's Hebrew classes and potential for growth.

The President's reference to the Chief Rabbi's superior knowledge about the immigrants, 'your experience of this class' indicates Swansea's typicality. The letter also reveals the immigrants' concern to promote the traditional, Jewish education of their children though they were prepared to accept the anglicisation of their children in the secular day school. The President's case was that for 1s per week the immigrants could have all privileges including education from the SHC. Instead, they preferred to pay up to 2s 6d per week presumably to fellow immigrant teachers to educate their children. The President regarded this as incomprehensible and perverse. From the immigrants' viewpoint, however, it reveals their own priorities in spending their limited income. Concerned about the education supplied by the SHC they opted to reduce contributions to that body and to provide their own instruction, an example of self-help. Indeed, with their own education and granted a *shochet*, they were almost an autonomous congregation. The defeat of a proposal for sexually segregated classes in the SHC's school provides a clue to their dissatisfaction (SHCA 1903: 25 Jan). When the immigrants established the BHM they instituted segregated classes for pupils over the age of 10 years. The preparedness of the Swansea's immigrants to adopt British culture but to retain control over Jewish education confirms Gartner's conclusion: 'Jewish parents displayed no discernible preference for Jewish schools over the State system so far as concerned general education. Immigrant Jewry did not greatly care who made Englishmen of their children, but they jealously guarded their right to make Jews of their children in their own way' (Gartner 1973: 231).

Although the Minutes Book does not indicate how peace was achieved in 1895 a separate immigrant congregation had emerged, first called 'the new Congregation' (SHCa 1899: 20 Jan), then 'the Prince of Wales Road Minyan' and eventually the *Bes Ha Midrash*, with its own building by 1906. In 1895 its spokesman was Mr D Rutter but in 1898 he renewed his membership of the SHC and the leader of the 'New Congregation' became Mr T Shepherd. In January 1899 Mr Shepherd wrote to the President of the SHC as follows:

> Considering the comparatively calm position between your Congregation and those (*sic*) to which I belong, I have taken the initiative and convinced our Congregation of the advisability of trying to reinstate the former good understanding which had hitherto existed before the establishment of the foreign Congregation.
>
> Probably you are aware that a good many of our Congregation pay towards yours also and only about 18 persons at most there is from whom your Congregation obtain no benefit and from these I propose to pay you an annual subscription of three pounds, providing you will let us have the privileges of the *shochet* and the Burial Ground. These are the principal and only conditions we put you. Should you require further details I shall be glad to hear from you when the meeting will take place. I would then attend personally. (SHC a1899: 20 Jan, recorded as deriving from 'the opposition congregation').

This letter shows that though a separate Congregation had been established there was still much cooperation, despite the talk of 'split', 'division', and 'opposition'. The overlapping membership of the two congregations suggests that the 'New Congregation' was relatively large, at least twice eighteen and probably many more. On behalf of the 18 non-contributors Mr Shepherd offered the sum of £3, similar to the agreements with small independent Congregations outside Swansea, for example Llanelli, Port Talbot, Ystalyfera, which became satellites of the SHC (Minutes Book for Agreements with Llanelli, Port Talbot and Ystalyfera).

A General Meeting of privileged members unanimously rejected Mr Shepherd's proposals and urged all his members to join the SHC and to pay a weekly subscription of 1s. By rejecting Mr Shepherd's offer of £3 the SHC was noting that the New Congregation differed from those outside the city boundaries. Moreover, economically £3 was insufficient to cover 18 members, each due to contribute £2s 12d per year.

After this rebuff an Extraordinary General Meeting was held on May 7 1899 'for the purpose of conferring with the dissidents for the object of arranging a settlement'. The meeting was truly 'extraordinary' since the Chief Rabbi occupied the Chair. No details of the discussions are supplied, apart from the Chief Rabbi's recommendation:

that the dissidents join the Congregation on the conditions "that the new Minister devotes full time to the Hebrew teaching of the children. In the event of the children largely exceeding 50, steps to be taken to engage an additional teacher. The supervision of the religious teaching to be vested in a Committee consisting of parents of the children and representatives of the Committee of the Congregation. Parents of children to pay not less than 1/- per week" (SHCa 1899: May).

It is clear that the issue separating the leaders of the SHC and the immigrants was control of the Hebrew education of the children. The Chief Rabbi wished the immigrant Congregation to amalgamate with the SHC and to pay its dues. As a concession the SHC was to establish a new education committee which included immigrants. This concession failed to meet their demands since 'The dissidents did not concur and the meeting terminated.' In a letter to A Lyons, President of SHC dated April 5 1899, he had said:

I am extremely anxious to use my best endeavours to induce the dissidents to return to your [word omitted]
I shall be glad if you will indicate to me such measures as you may deem advisable to be taken with my regard to meeting the dissidents.

This rejection stemmed from the fact that Dr Adler's solution favoured the SHC who wished to retain control over the dissidents through their subscriptions to the Congregation. Indeed the Chief Rabbi had colluded with the President of the SHC about how to handle the forthcoming meeting.

Education was so important to the immigrants that even the Chief Rabbi was unable to convince them to become full SHC members, though a majority of them paid it some subscription. Unfortunately, apart from segregated classes, we do not know why they were dissatisfied with the SHC's education - perhaps too English, not sufficiently traditional, inferior - but clearly they sought to control the education and the Jewishness of their children who were subject to rapid cultural changes in Britain.

The position however changed later that year with the appointment of a new minister, Reverend Simon Fyne, born in Kovno, who held a teaching certificate from Jews' College, London (Mars *in press*). As an immigrant minister with a British education and an early Zionist activist, Reverend Fyne was similar in background to the newcomers. Leading members of the new Congregation expressed satisfaction with his appointment and promised to subscribe to the Congregation and to allow Reverend Fyne to educate their children (SHCa 1899: Oct).

Despite satisfaction with Reverend Fyne the New Congregation or the Prince of Wales Minyan continued to exist and seemed about to establish itself as a separate congregation:

The President read a lengthy communication received by him reporting the result of a meeting held at the Temperance Hall on the 29th convened by the Swansea Jewish Watch Committee (T Shepherd in the Chair) for the purpose of establishing a New Congregation and Talmud Torah apart from and independent of the one known as the Swansea Hebrew Congregation. (SHCa 1902: Jan)

The Committee's reply was 'that no notice be officially taken of the communication'

It seems likely that the Swansea Jewish Watch Committee was identical with the Prince of Wales Road Minyan, for when the latter requested the Reverend Fyne's services on the second day of Pentecost, the request was granted provided that the services were held in a suitable place and that the PWM did not enrol members eligible for the SHC (SHCa 1902: Jan).

Clearly, the SHC was prepared to cooperate provided the PWM did not compete for recruits. Later that year both organisations arranged services on the High Festivals under the aegis of the SHC whereby affiliates of the PWM paid '1s per seat including a Lady's seat if required, and all others a minimum of 2s 6d each.'

The two groups failed to agree on joint services in 1903, though the SHC allowed Reverend Fyne to deliver a sermon in the Albert Hall to the PWM on the Day of Atonement. In 1904 Wardens of the PWM again requested joint arrangements for the High Festivals similar to the agreement of 1902. At a Committee meeting of the SHC attended by the wardens of the PWM, recognition of the latter as a respectable, organised body was granted when:

It was unanimously resolved that the Prince of Wales Road Minyan arrange the overflow services on their own account and that the sum of three guineas be granted them from the funds of the Congregation towards the expenses of same. The Congregation to have the right of sending any poor people to the services free of charge.' (SHCa 1904)

In 1905 however, when the PWM sought to repeat the arrangement the SHC refused, though a few months earlier Reverend Fyne had been released to conduct a service and deliver a sermon at the PWM during Passover.

Early in 1906 the PWM gave way to the *Bes Ha Midrash*, first mentioned in the Minutes Book of the SHC on June 10 1906, when the BHM sought to send four representatives to the SHC Committee meeting to discuss the building of the BHM synagogue. Subsequently the request of the Secretary of the BHM for the services of Reverend Lubner at laying the foundation stone of the BHM was granted (SHCa 1906).

The relationship between the SHC and the new BHM was friendly, marked by a spirit of cooperation, manifest in a letter from Mr A Levy, Chairman of the Building Committee of the BHM, in which he solicited financial assistance from the SHC and clearly pointed out that his organisation did not intend to compete with it. As proof, he quoted from the Trust Deeds of the BHM:

> that the Beth Ha Midrash shall work in harmony with the existing Hebrew Congregation in the borough of Swansea, and should any dispute or disputes arise between the Beth Ha Midrash and the Hebrew Congregation, such dispute or disputes shall be settled by the decision of the Chief Rabbi of Great Britain.'(SHCa 1907: 6 Jan)

So harmonious were these links that a donation of ten guineas was made by the SHC to the BHM, and three years after its creation, the President of the BHM, Mr A Levy, informed the SHC that he was authorised to propose amalgamation with the SHC (SHCa 1909). Subsequent discussions between the two groups modified amalgamation to affiliation, along the lines of congregations outside Swansea such as Aberavon and Llanelli. At a General Meeting of the SHC on July 10 1909 the following resolution from the Committee was unanimously passed:

> that this Committee recommend to the members of the SHC the affiliation of the Beth Ha Midrash, as a community to this Congregation for one year subject to their paying to this Congregation 20 per annum, payable quarterly in advance. The BHM in turn to be entitled to the services of the officials of this Congregation on the occasion of any Births, Deaths or Marriages, occurring in their community, unless otherwise required by this Congregation and also to include the right of allotment of ground for burial in the cemetery at Swansea subject to the rules for the time being of this Congregation.

This agreement was accepted by the President of the BHM, Mr A Levy and is recorded in the Minutes of the SHC for August 24 1909. The willingness of the SHC to assist the BHM was manifest early in 1912 when the BHM had recruited a Rabbi, a Russian immigrant, but were experiencing difficulties in paying his salary. The SHC wrote to the BHM and offered £15 per annum, provided the latter contributed a similar amount (BHM 1912: 11 Jan).

The creation of the BHM and its recognition by the SHC as a separate yet satellite community represented a bowing to the inevitable. The immigrants, whose numbers had continued to increase, wished to determine their own affairs especially in the sphere of education, and they were unwilling to become subscribers without political rights. However, they accepted the authority of the Chief Rabbi as arbitrator in disputes between the two communities and acknowledged the institutional and corporate strength of the SHC as manifest in its access to personnel and burial ground.

The privileged members of the SHC who had proved unable or unwilling to democratise their organisation to accommodate the newcomers nevertheless provided services for them. Indeed, as fellow Jews but especially as 'English' Jews, they championed the continued immigration of

Swansea Talmud Torah, Cheder Session 1908-9.

Swansea Talmud Cheder Session 1908-9 (reprinted by permission of Mr Martin Glass). Note the contrast in clothing with the photograph on page 128.

Russian and Eastern European Jews against opposition that resulted in the passing of the Aliens Act of 1905 (cf Gainer 1972 for a discussion of this Act). Thus on May 5 1904 the President of the SHC, Mr Hyam Goldberg, wrote a letter to his Swansea MP and to those of neighbouring constituencies in which he objected to the Act as it proceeded through Parliament, on the grounds that it was 'un-English in character' since it penalised the victims of religious persecution. The leaders of the SHC also joined with the editor of the South Wales *Daily News*, David Davies, to launch a public appeal to assist victims of the Kishinev pogroms of 1905 (£210 8s 6d was raised *Jewish Chronicle* 5 Jan 1906).

The SHC's recognition of the BHM shifted the relationship from one of government and 'opposition' or 'dissidents' to one of toleration and cooperation. The two were now separate, certainly not equal, but linked together. The area of ethnicity marks their conjunction and disjunction. Each recognised the other as Jews and each acknowledged the authority of the Chief Rabbi, a move which represented a marked acculturation by the immigrants. But how did these two groups perceive each other? For the immigrants, the SHC was the 'English' synagogue, whereas for the SHC the immigrants were the 'foreigners', and not only 'foreign', but also poor and working-class. Leaders of the SHC saw themselves, and were seen by the immigrants, as Englishmen, the newcomers remained foreign but many of them maintained membership of both institutions.

The BHM's establishment as a separate congregation absolved the SHC from democratising its constitution and organisation. Attempts to do so had been made in the past, for example, in an endeavour to reduce the powers of the privileged members David Seline, a solicitor, and the son of I. Seline, both privileged members, proposed in July 1905 that all members who had paid 1s per week for twelve months should be granted privileged membership and entitled to vote at General Meetings. This proposal, defeated by 16 votes to 10, may have hastened the formation of the BHM. David Seline, who became President of the SHC in 1909, did not continue with reforms and may have faced obstacles had he persisted since the more successful immigrant members had achieved that privileged status, whilst their poorer co-religionists, who might have allied with them, were now affiliated to their own congregation, the BHM.

The members of the BHM, rapidly acculturated to British society. For example, records of committee meetings and general meetings were kept in English (their minutes date from 1910, but are not as full as those of the SHC nor include balance sheets); concern with decorum and proper behaviour were urged, thus one member was expelled in November 1915:

> after past troubles the Congregation having had from him and having lost good members through him, it was unanimously agreed to have him *expelled* [emphasis in original] on November 28 1915 and that if he at any time visits the Synagogue as a visitor, he shall behave himself, as a gentleman and a real Jew, failing the police be sent for and order him out, and should he try any disturbance at the Synagogue again that police court proceedings be taken against him for to reject him of coming to the synagogue and obtain by the magistrates an order for him to keep the peace with the officials of the congregation.' (BHM 1912; the expulsee had had a previous warning).

In this case we see that the immigrant community had quickly acquired the notion of the gentleman and had coupled it with conduct befitting a 'real Jew', implying that the expulsee's behaviour was anything but Jewish. In addition the door was literally left open to the recalcitrant to return but only as a visitor. The strong sanction of expulsion was reinforced by the threat to summon the police, an institution eschewed by Jews in Eastern Europe and loath to invoke in Britain except under extreme provocation. Acceptance of the police and the state as the ultimate sanction indicates an ever increasing self-confidence in British society by this community and also the revulsion they felt at the offence. The late Mr Joseph Goldberg, a warden of the SHC, formerly member of the *Bes Ha Midrash*, informed me that the immigrants believed the police had the power to deport criminal, immigrant Jews. Hence, informing the police was a powerful sanction.

E. Barnett. A. Deggots. A. Rubenstein.   M. Jacobs.   A. Lyons.   I. Seline.   M. L. Marks.   I. R. Levi. H. Goldberg.
  H. Barnett.   A. Freedman   Dd. Seline   Rev. M. Lubner   Very Rev. Dr. H. Adler   Miss N. Adler   Rev. H. J. Sandheim
                (*Treasurer*).   (*President*).   (*Reader*).   (*Chief Rabbi*).   (*Minister*).

Jubilee of the Swansea Synagogue, May 1909, showing the leaders of the SHC with the Chief Rabbi and his daughter

One area where the BHM reflected, indeed replicated, its parent, the SHC, was its fee structure. In February 1916 the Committee of the BHM 'agreed to classify seats according to contributions, i.e. 3d seats at the rear, 6d centre, and 9d top seats'. All 6d or less members excluded from privileges of the English Congregation and 3d members to have no vote and be excluded from meetings' (BHM 1961).

Not only had the BHM adopted a ranking system similar to the SHC but the two congregations became united in a single Swansea Jewish community that shared the burial ground, arrangements for kosher meat, the *mikveh*, and the services of the ministers of the SHC. The stratification system within Swansea's Jewish community persisted but in a modified form. These two synagogues, each with its own officers and educational arrangements, now served the needs of a single community but instead of a sharp caste-like situation that had obtained earlier, a single, but differentiated class system had emerged. At the top of this community came the privileged members of the SHC, below them the 1s 6d seatholders and lower still the 1s subscribers. The highest 9d subscribers to the BHM enjoyed access to the privileges of the SHC and straddled the two congregations, the 6d members were enfranchised with the BHM, at the bottom were the disenfranchised 3d members.

The destruction in 1941 of the Goat Street Synagogue by German bombs produced attempts to merge the SHC and the BHM. In 1955 a new synagogue was built in Ffynone, Swansea, and members of both groups formed a single congregation in the new building. The BHM continued to exist even though its members had joined the new synagogue but it was dissolved in 1961 and its assets were transferred to a synagogue in Israel, known as the Bes Ma Midrash Netiv Meir.

The ultimate fusion of the two congregations can be seen in the election as Wardens of the SHC in 1984 of two men, the late Mr Monty Black whose father was a founder of the BHM and the late Mr Joe Goldberg, whose father was an early member of the BHM.

Bibliography

Alderman G 1972 'The Anti-Jewish Riots of August 1911 in South Wales', *Welsh History Review*, 6: 190-200.

Alderman G 1979 'The Jew as Scapegoat?: the Settlement and Reception of Jews in South Wales before 1914', *Transactions of the Jewish Historical Society of England*, 26: 62-70.

BHM 1910-61 'Beth Ha Midrash Minute Book' Swansea: Swansea Hebrew Congregation.

Collins K 1987 'Aspects of Scottish Jewry', Glasgow Jewish Representative Council.

Encyclopaedia Judaica 1970.

Gainer B 1972 *The Alien Invasion*, London: Heinemann.

Gartner L P 1973 *The Jewish Immigrant in England 1870-1914*, London: Simon Publications (first edition 1960).

Gartner L P 1981 'Urban History and the Pattern of Provincial Jewish Settlement in Victorian England', *Jewish Journal of Sociology*, 23: 37-55.

Gartner L P 1986 'A Quarter Century of Anglo-Jewish Historiography', *Jewish Social Studies*, 48: 105-126.

Goldblum B 1975 Paper on Swansea's Jewish community presented at Conference on Provincial Jewry in Victorian Britain convened by the Jewish Historical Society of England.

Henriques U 1988 'The Jewish Community of Cardiff 1813-1914', *The Welsh History Review*,14: 269-300.

Josephs Z 1980 *Birmingham Jewry 1749-1914*, Birmingham.

Josephs Z 1984 *Birmingham Jewry Vol.II More Aspects, 1740-1930*, Birmingham.

Kokosolakis, N 1982 *Ethnic Identity and Religion: Tradition and Change in Liverpool Jewry*, Washington: University Press of America.

Levin S S (ed) 1970 *A Century of Jewish Life, 1870-1970*, London,

Mars, L (in press) 'The Ministry of the Reverend Simon Fyne in Swansea, 1899-1906', *Jewish Social Studies.*

Saunders, N H 1980 'Swansea Hebrew Congregation, 1730-1980', 250th Anniversary volume, Swansea.

Shaftesbury, J M 1970 'Religious Controversies' in Levin 1970.

Sharot, S 1976 **Judaism: A Sociology**, London: David and Charles.

Swansea Bes Ha Midrash *Minutes Book 1910-1961.*

SHCa 1895-1909 'Swansea Hebrew Congregation Minute Book'.

SHCb 1892 'Swansea Hebrew Congregation: Rule Book'.

SHCc 1902-1904 'Swansea Hebrew Congregation: Letters Book'.

Williams B 1976 *The Making of Manchester Jewry 1740-1875*, Manchester: Manchester University Press.

11
Mapping Church Decline

Robin Gill

One of the many paradoxes of the sociology of religion as it has developed over the last twenty years is that it has given more attention to sects or new religious movements than it has to long-established denominations or churches. With important exceptions (e.g. Hornsby-Smith 1987) the latter have not received the sort of detailed attention that one might expect given their prevalence and size. In part this may be due to lingering suspicions of 'Religious Sociology' and to the ecclesiastical control often thought to lurk behind it in France. It may also be due to the sheer difficulty of analysing amorphous religious institutions. Small scale religious bodies are more sociologically controllable at both levels. Whatever the reason, long-established churches remain relatively unresearched. Even when sociologists have shown an interest in churches they have typically relied upon generalised data (Currie, Gilbert and Horsley 1977). Invaluable as it is as a source of historical information about national church membership, it is notoriously lacking in information about Sunday-by-Sunday churchgoing as such and tends to put forward variables related to general church decline in a highly impressionistic manner. And the now vast literature on secularization frequently avoids statistical data altogether: or else it uses *both* statistics related to church decline in Europe and statistics showing persisting but supposedly epiphenomenal churchgoing in the States as indications of secularization (Wilson 1966, 1976; see also my review of recent literature, Gill 1989).

In contrast, a number of recent social historians have shown a developing interest in churches as social phenomena. Stephen Yeo's detailed study of Reading in the 19th and early twentieth centuries is already well known to sociologists of religion (1976). Rather less well known is Cox (1982), Obelkevich (1976), and Brown (1987). Together they suggest that there is considerably more data available on churches as social phenomena than is often imagined and that this data is directly relevant to understanding the decline of most British churches throughout the twentieth century. Far from being generalised studies, they each show that an intense analysis of churches in a confined area (even Brown's study is highly concentrated upon Glasgow and parts of the Borders) yields insights that cannot be deduced from national church membership statistics.

What emerges from this, I believe, is the realisation that such intense study of churches at a local level is a prerequisite for understanding the social factors that affect them. This in itself would be a standard premise in the sociological study of sects or new religious movements. Ever since the 1950s, and in particular Wilson (1955; see also Gill 1989), the detailed local study of small-scale religious bodies has been preferred to generalised discussions of them as national, or international, institutions. Presumably this is based upon the realisation that national information is often partisan and may not accurately represent the way a body functions in practice.

But this applies *a fortiori* to churches. The claims that a church makes at a national level may or may not be based upon the way it functions in practice at the local level. Indeed, part of the skill of the social scientist involves comparing claims with actual behaviour. To make such comparisons there is no substitute for detailed empirical research and it has, perhaps, been the most signal failing of the literature on secularization that it has seldom been based upon such research.

It is on these premises that my own research over five years on church decline is based. It focuses specifically on the North East of England (principally Northumberland) and is an attempt to produce an empirical map of churches there which isolates the factors responsible for their decline. This chapter is written after a year of this research and offers an indication of the directions that it has already taken and, more briefly, may take over the remaining four years.

The pilot study for my research (Gill 1989) has involved an extended analysis of fourteen adjacent parishes in North Northumberland. Together they represent one of the most deeply rural parts of England, with the Scottish Border to their North and West and contain no town much larger than 2,000 people at any point since 1801. They stop well short of Alnwick to the South and Berwick-upon-Tweed and the coast to the East. In 1801 the total population of this area was 13,971, at its height in 1851 it was 17,557, and today it is just 7,070: there has been continuous depopulation since 1851. It thus offers the sociologist a highly rural comparator for the intensely urban areas that characterise the South of the county.

This was an area which experienced considerable Border warfare up to the seventeenth century (most notably Flodden Field in 1513), but which has subsequently been rich farming land. To study the physical presence of churches in it I divided history since the restoration of the monarchy (when church records become more available) into four equal periods of time: 1661-1740; 1741-1820; 1821-1900; 1901-1980.

In the first period the Church of England was particularly active. In nine of the fourteen parishes an incumbent became resident and a new vicarage was built for him. One church was enlarged and nine others were renovated. In addition seven Dissenting (using the term technically simply to denote non-established denominations) chapels/churches were built, one was enlarged and four manses were built.

In the second period, nine Church of England churches were renovated, five enlarged and one further parish received a resident incumbent, with a vicarage built for him. In addition, four Dissenting churches were built, four were enlarged, and six new manses were built.

The third period was the busiest of all. In it all but one of the fourteen Church of England parishes renovated their parish church, all but two built new vicarages, seven additional chapels or missions halls were built, and all the parishes now had their own resident incumbent. Three of the parishes had total populations of less that 300 and, in the case of one of these, of less than 200. Further, fifteen new Dissenting churches were built, three were enlarged, six were renovated, and seven new manses were built. Yet ironically this period experienced continuous depopulation from 1851.

This depopulation characterised the whole of the fourth period. No new churches were built or enlarged - although seven Church of England churches were renovated, three vicarages were built and three Dissenting churches were renovated. However, uniquely in this period, in eight Church of England parishes the incumbents ceased to be resident and their vicarages were sold, four mission halls were sold, and thirteen Dissenting churches and eleven manses were sold.

Using the returns from the 1851 Religious Census it would appear that altogether the churches and chapels in the area had 11,034 seats (sufficient for 63% of the total population and, in reality far more, since some of the parishioners would have been quite small!). Yet, despite continuous depopulation churches continued to build right up to the end of the nineteenth century. On the basis of the 1851 Religious Census (and subsequent local estimates for additional or enlarged church buildings) by 1901 there would have been 13,049 seats for a total population of only 10,970. Of these seats the Dissenters had 8,704 and the Church of England 4,345. Further, an excess of church seating capacity over total population characterised this area from the 1890s until the 1970s.

Unless there was a dramatic rise in churchgoing between 1851 and 1901, churches which were only 49.3% occupied at the main service on Mothering Sunday in 1851 must have been considerably emptier (despite folk memories) by 1901. If the churchgoing rate had stayed steady, the dual effects of depopulation and increased church seating would have resulted in only 22.1% of these seats being occupied at the main service on a comparable Sunday in 1901. If the churchgoing rate had declined the situation would clearly have been considerably worse. Even if there had been a dramatic increase it would have had to have reached 58% of the total population for churches to have appeared as full (but no more) as they were in 1851.

A detailed study of Visitation Returns to the Bishop of Durham in 1866, 1874 and 1878, and to the Bishop of Newcastle in 1887, suggests that average attendances in the Church of England reached their peak in 1866 and declined thereafter. The 1851 Religious Census asked incumbents to estimate actual attendances on Mothering Sunday and average adult church attendances. If the latter are used, aggregated average attendances for the area were 2,342 in 1851 (13.3% of the total population), 2,884 in 1866 (17.6% pop), 2,237 in 1874 (15.0% pop), 2,437 in 1878 (16.3% pop) and 2,039 in 1887 (15.0% pop). Further, attendances in 1887 at the main service at the three largest churches in the area were estimated to be only half those of 1851. In other words, less actual attendances were spread over more church buildings.

A very similar pattern emerges from the detailed study of Presbyterian Communion Rolls and attendances (where available), average attendances at Mass at the three Catholic churches in the area, and membership records of the five small Primitive Methodist chapels. Each showed a pattern of expansion, followed by a slow reduction of attendance/membership, concluding with the closure of church buildings and the loss of a resident minister/priest. Perhaps surprisingly, Catholics contracted first: their combined Easter Mass attendances were 234 in 1849, 480 in 1855, but had declined to 297 in 1861, to 187 in 1892 and to just 109 in 1899. Presbyterian churches characteristically reached a peak of Communion Roll membership in the 1860s or 1870s, and then declined rapidly, closing their first major church (seating over 1,000) in 1903. The Primitive Methodists had a much smaller membership, which expanded later, reaching a highpoint of 260 in 1888, but reducing to 160 by 1908 and closing all but two of its chapels by the 1980s.

Real, and not just perceived, decline in attendances has now characterised all of the churches in the area. A census that I conducted of the remaining 29 churches of all denominations (out of 45 in 1901) at Pentecost 1988 suggested that there were 636 attendances of all ages (9.0% pop). On Mothering Sunday in 1851 there were estimated to be 5,436 attendances at morning services (31.0% pop: afternoon/evening services represented just 7.9%).

From a detailed analysis of these declining rural churches it has been possible to isolate three factors which directly relate to this phenomenon of over-capacity in the context of ongoing depopulation and which can be identified as causal factors in church decline. The first of these is the actual closing of churches. Each of the four denominations has closed churches. The Presbyterians, who constituted three-quarters of churchgoers in the area in 1851, but now less than half, have closed the most. By examining those Communion Rolls which also record individual attendances it is possible to map out the way individuals respond to a church closure. Characteristically, membership and attendance diminish rapidly as closure nears, only half of the remaining members actually transfer to a neighbouring church after closure and then are significantly less regular in their attendance at the new church than they were at the old.

The second factor involves a change in relationship between ministers and congregations. If in 1851 there was one church per minister, in the 1980s there are three churches per minister (across denominations). The ratio of population to minister has changed rather less: in 1851 there were 605 people per minister, in the 1980s there are 707 per minister. However multiple charges now characterise all denominations (although the Catholics are currently reducing their three churches to one). Leslie Francis's empirical research suggests that ministers with three or more churches become significantly less effective and their congregations reduce accordingly (1985).

The third factor is small, and increasingly elderly, congregations in large, empty church buildings. In one church, which seats some 500, there is now a congregation of five. And none of the other churches were remotely full at Pentecost 1988. It is not difficult to see that it is today more difficult for the marginal churchgoers to attend church (without feeling too conspicuous) than it was in 1851. A measure of this change is the changed ratio between Easter communions and average attendances on other Sundays. In the Church of England quarterly Communions represented just 2.1% of the total population in 1810-14, 2.2% in 1857, 1.8% in 1887, but in 1986 Easter Communions represented 9.4%. But in 1986 this was over twice estimated average attendances (3.6% pop), whereas in the 1850s it represented just 17% of aggregated average attendances. Similarly amongst Presbyterians today, quarterly communions represent at least double average congregations, whereas in the 1850s they were slightly less than aggregated average attendances. In both instances it may be the less committed church members (i.e. the non-communicants) who are now largely absent from public worship.

The next stage of my research has involved asking two questions. First, why did churches continue to build in the face of depopulation and their own evident decline? Second, did this phenomenon of overcapacity - leading to church closures, shared ministers, and sparse, elderly congregations - happen elsewhere in rural Britain?

To answer the first question I have been examining in detail the written records left by the four denominations. What emerges is a very considerable degree of inter-church rivalry. The Bishop of Durham's questions in 1810 and 1814 to his clergy show that he was as concerned about the presence of 'Papists' as of Dissenters: 'Are there any reputed Papists in your Parish or Chapelry? How many, and of what Rank? Have any persons been lately perverted to Popery?' (Clergy Visitation Returns). The clergy responses from North Northumberland show instead that they were predominantly concerned about the Presbyterians. By 1861 the Bishop of Durham dropped all reference to 'Papists', but not questions about Dissenters. In response one incumbent wrote, in terms similar to those of others: 'The special hindrance to ministerial success in all the Border Parishes is the lamentable extent of Presbyterian Dissent.' Indeed, throughout the second half of the nineteenth century the Church of England continued to write about the 'threat' of Presbyterianism. So, in 1891, the Bishop of Newcastle asked: 'What are the chief hindrances to the success of your Pastoral labours?' One incumbent responded bluntly: 'The struggle of Dissenters to keep their Ministers: dislike to Forms of Prayer: jealousy of Church: deep prejudice: neglect in the past.'

Ironically, Presbyterians in the area very seldom referred to 'Episcopalians' as they termed them. Instead their rivalries were chiefly with each other. Schisms within particular congregations went back at least to the eighteenth century. However the Scottish Disruption of 1843 created enormous tension amongst local congregations, resulting in several new and rival churches being built in the decade following 1848. Normally prosaic Session minutes became quite animated and, in one case, physical violence erupted within a congregation.

Catholic records in turn suggest that those in authority believed that they were bringing salvation to the area for the first time since the Dissolution. Records assiduously counted 'converts' and churches were described as 'missions'. In an area which already had very evident inter-church rivalries, Catholics and then Primitive Methodists brought more. The strength of these rivalries does seem to explain why they all continued to build in a context of depopulation, even when their own relative decline must have become first apparent. Indeed, the 'mission halls' built by Anglicans in the 1890s were specifically designed to counter decline, in the belief that people did not come to church because the parish church was too far from the people. In reality they must have drawn away even more people from parish churches which were already experiencing real decline.

But did this happen elsewhere? To answer this question I have been examining the seating capacity of the churches for each Registration District in England and Wales given in the 1851 Religious Census against the population figures for the same Districts for 1901. Rather surprisingly this simple exercise reveals that in 84 Registration Districts (out of 623) the seating capacity of the churches in existence in 1851 would have exceeded the 1901 population. Such was the extent of rural depopulation in England and Wales in the second half of the nineteenth century In no less than 178 Districts there would have room in 1901 for over 80% of the population. So, without allowing for any extra church building in rural areas after 1851 (despite abundant evidence that such building did take place), there would already have been a very considerable problem of over-capacity by the end of the century.

Obelkevich's study of South Lindsey misses this crucial point. He sets out very usefully the rivalries between Methodists and Anglicans in the area and the degree to which both built in the context of depopulation. Yet he finally puzzles about why churches there were in decline by 1870. Had he examined the seating of the churches in the 1851 Religious Census against the 1901 population for Horncastle, Spilsby and Louth, he might have discovered. In 1851 there was already seating capacity in all of the churches there for 89.9% of the total population. The Church of England alone could have accommodated 43.1% of the population (its average nationally was 29.7%). But by 1901, without any additional churches, the Church of England could have accommodated 52.0% of the population and all the church together 108.4% of the same population. In such circumstances church closures, shared ministers and persisting sparse congregations seem inescapable.

Most remarkably of all, the adjacent Registration Districts of Leyburn, Askrigg and Reeth in North Riding, already had seating capacity for their 1851 population of 105.7%. By 1901 the same churches could have accommodated 172.8% of the population and by 1971 no less than 225.1% of the population. Not surprisingly in 1851, although 30.2% of the population were at the main service on Mothering Sunday, they occupied just 28.5% of available church seating. By 1901 the same churchgoing rate would have filled only 17.5% of available seating.

The 1851 Religious Census also supplies abundant evidence of inter-church rivalry. In every Registration District throughout England and Wales several rival denominations were present. In Askrigg, out of 33 church buildings only 6 belonged to the Church of England: the Independents (Congregationalists) had 9, the Wesleyan Methodists 8, and the Primitive Methodists 3. And so throughout the Country. Indeed the rate of church building was accelerating (only in part due to the challenge of urbanisation): between 1801 and 1811 1,224 new churches were built; another 2,002 were built by 1821; 3,141 by 1831; 4,866 by 1841; and 5,594 by 1851.

Taken together this research suggests that rural churches had a massive problem by 1901 - from which they are still trying to recover. Overcapacity, a product of inter-church rivalry in a context of rural depopulation, appears widespread. For those churches which lacked a substantial rural subsidy (i.e. the non-Anglican churches) it has proved disastrous. The closure of Dissenting churches must have characterised much of rural England and Wales throughout the twentieth century. Even the Church of England has been forced to amalgamate livings and return to the clerical pluralism of the eighteenth century.

The next stage of my research will be to examine churches in relation population changes in Newcastle upon Tyne. Naturally the population shifts there were quite opposite (although extensive depopulation did characterise the centre of London during the second half of the nineteenth century). It will be just as important to examine each of the denominations in detail as they sought to respond to massive immigration. They clearly did not react in identical manners. For example, Catholics in Newcastle currently have about twice as many average attendances as Anglicans, yet the latter have four times as many church buildings. Further, there are indications from Clergy Returns that a number of the older, city-centre Anglican churches were already struggling by the 1870s, even though general levels of Anglican churchgoing may have held fairly steady until at least the 1880s.

Once this stage of the research is complete the next will be to produce a total map of the churches in Northumberland, looking for variations between rural, urban and suburban areas over the 19th and 20th centuries. A sufficiently large data base should allow for these comparisons to be made across denominations. Again the stress will be upon statistical data, although clearly other forms of data must also be taken into consideration (as I have already indicated). Eventually it must also include more elusive groups, such as the House Church Movement. Another aspect which will require attention is the involvement of the churches in the wider community - the study of which Yeo and Cox have done much to pioneer. Only from careful and meticulous analysis can results be finally expected. However, together the comparative data should eventually be able to supply a map of the institutional churches in the North East of England which can generate insights for churches elsewhere in Britain. That, at least, is my hope.

Bibliography

Brown, C 1987 *The Social History of Religion in Scotland Since 1730*, London: Methuen.

Clergy Visitation Returns, 1810 *Auckland Castle Episcopal Records for the Diocese of Durham*, University of Durham, Department of Palaeography and Diplomatic, University of Durham.

Clergy Visitation Returns 1882 Diocese of Newcastle, Gosforth: Northumberland Record Office.

Cox, J 1982 *The English Churches in a Secular Society: Lambeth 1970-1930*, Oxford: Oxford University Press.

Currie, R, Gilbert, A and Horsley, L 1977 *Churches and Churchgoers*, Cambridge: Cambridge University Press.

Francis, L J 1985 *Rural Anglicanism*, London: Collins.

Gill, R 1989 *Competing Convictions*, London: SCM Press.

Hornsby-Smith, M P 1987 *Roman Catholics in England*, Cambridge University Press.

Obelkevitch, J 1976 *Religion and Rural Society: South Lindsey 1825-1875*, Oxford: Oxford University Press.

Yeo, S 1976 *Religion and Voluntary Organisations in Crisis*, London: Croom Helm.

Wilson, B R 1955 *Sects and Society*, London: Heinemann.

Wilson, B R 1966 *Religion in Secular Society*,London: Watts.

Wilson, B R 1976 *Contemporary Transformations of Religion*, Oxford: Oxford University Press.

Index